asian-inspired
MACHINE EMBROIDERY

Joan Elliott

KRAUSE PUBLICATIONS
CINCINNATI, OHIO

www.fwmedia.com

14   13   12   11   10   5   4   3   2   1

DISTRIBUTED IN CANADA BY FRASER DIRECT
100 Armstrong Avenue
Georgetown, ON, Canada L7G 5S4
Tel: (905) 877-4411

DISTRIBUTED IN THE U.K. AND EUROPE BY DAVID & CHARLES
Brunel House, Newton Abbot, Devon, TQ12 4PU, England
Tel: (+44) 1626 323200, Fax: (+44) 1626 323319
Email: postmaster@davidandcharles.co.uk

DISTRIBUTED IN AUSTRALIA BY CAPRICORN LINK
P.O. Box 704, S. Windsor NSW, 2756 Australia
Tel: (02) 4577-3555

Library of Congress Cataloging in Publication Data
Elliott, Joan
  Asian-Inspired Machine Embroidery/ by Joan Elliott.--
    1st ed.
      p. cm.
  Includes index.
  ISBN-13: 978-0-89689-954-4 (pbk. : alk. paper)
  1. Embroidery, Machine--Patterns. 2. Embroidery--
    Asia--Themes, motives. I. Title.
  TT772.E44 2010
  746.44'041--dc22   2010001227

Editor: Nancy Breen

Technical Editor: Rebecca Kemp Brent

Designer: Steven Peters

Cover Designer: Rachael Smith

Production Coordinator: Greg Nock

Photographer: Ric Deliantoni

Stylist: Lauren Emmerling

Freelance Art Director: Karla Baker

Metric Conversion Chart

To convert	to	multiply by
Inches	Centimeters	2.54
Centimeters	Inches	0.4
Feet	Centimeters	30.5
Centimeters	Feet	0.03
Yards	Meters	0.9
Meters	Yards	1.1

DEDICATION
For Geri and Jay, with love and thanks for all you have taught me.

ACKNOWLEDGEMENTS

Working on this book has given me the opportunity to meet and collaborate with many very talented people.

Thank you to Candy Wiza and Jay Staten, who first proposed adding a book of machine embroidery designs to my repertoire.

To Nancy Breen, my editor, my heartfelt thanks for your guidance, patience and encouragement.

To Jay Fishman, my digitizer, and Geri Finio, my embroiderer, your help and support this past year were invaluable. You never cease to amaze me with your talents and expertise.

Thanks go to Baby Lock for providing me with their wonderful embroidery machine, and to Robison-Anton and Sulky for the threads and stabilizers used in all the projects.

Finally, to the design staff at Krause, many thanks for a job well done.

Table of Contents

Introduction

The art of embroidery has been a treasured tradition in Asian culture for centuries. Daily life and creative talents merged beautifully in both Japan and China. A wonderful connection to the natural world developed and was reflected in fashion, art and all the aesthetic disciplines. Artisans captured nature's beauty in detail, combining the finest silks in luxurious colors with the most delicate stitches.

Machine embroidery seems the perfect medium for bringing these traditions into our own lives. If you do hand embroidery instead, don't worry—all of the designs are available as black and white line drawings on the CD-ROM that accompanies this book so you can create your own embroidery transfers.

My own interest in Chinese and Japanese art gave birth to the designs in this book. Drawing inspiration from Japanese woodblock prints, hand-painted silk fans, calligraphy and opulent silk kimonos, I've put together a collection of designs and projects that will bring a taste of Asian elegance to your creations.

With a nod to the lovely seasonal blossoms found in Japanese gardens, I've designed some regal irises, magnificent magnolias, lush peonies, fragrant cherry blossoms and brilliant poppies for you to embroider. Use them to decorate a variety of projects: an easy-to-make bookmark, a fashionable silk scarf, cheerful spring table linens and an eyelet-edged handkerchief. Add the classic image of a pretty silk fan to a brocade blouse to give your wardrobe a lovely Asian touch.

As a passionate gardener, I couldn't resist including a chapter with some of my favorite flowers to embroider on all of the necessary gardening accessories. Peonies, plum blossoms, chrysanthemums and bluebells dance across a cheerful gardener's apron, visor and tote. For the little ones, or maybe for the child in you, you'll find a set of playful pandas to stitch onto a cozy afghan, pillow and matching nightgown.

Celebrate the changing seasons with projects featuring my four colorful kimono designs. My geisha portrait, reminiscent of elegant Japanese woodblock prints, can be used as an insert for the back of a hand mirror. Shimmering koi and dragonflies grace terry towels and matching slippers—a chic bath set to create from ready-made blanks.

You can incorporate your embroidery easily into some charming handmade cards. I've styled some calligraphic kanji symbols for sending wishes of happiness and peace. There are also two radiant butterfly cards for conveying personal messages.

Tips on supplies and techniques for both machine and hand embroidery are included. Easy-to-follow instructions accompany all of the projects.

Multiple designs presented throughout many of the chapters allow you to mix and match as you please. Use your imagination to design projects that are uniquely yours.

Join me in this Asian-themed adventure and set your creative spirit free!

Getting Started

If you are an experienced embroiderer, I hope you can use the designs in this book and on the CD-ROM in many different ways. If you are new to this wonderful craft, this section offers basic information to help you get started.

If you are lucky enough to have an embroidery machine dealer nearby, take advantage of any demonstrations, lectures and classes the shop holds. Hands-on learning is always a great help, and you will become part of an embroidery community where you can share ideas and show off your latest creations.

See *Further Reading* on this page for a list of books that provide more in-depth instruction on machine embroidery. As with most handiwork, the more you do, the easier the process gets, so don't be afraid to try new stabilizers, fabrics and threads. Most importantly, have fun with your machine as you explore the Asian-inspired designs in this book.

If you're doing this book's designs in hand embroidery, please see *Tips for Hand Embroidery* on page 16 and *Embroidery Stitches* on page 18. You'll find information about transferring designs from the CD-ROM to your fabric and advice about tools and materials as well as stitching suggestions.

Further Reading

The Embroidery Stitch Bible
by Betty Barnden

Fill in the Blanks with Machine Embroidery
by Rebecca Kemp Brent

Machine Embroidery on Difficult Materials
by Deborah Jones

Machine Embroidery Wild & Wacky
by Linda Turner Griepentrog and
Rebecca Kemp Brent

Machine Embroidery with Confidence
by Nancy Zieman

All books by Krause Publications
(see www.mycraftivitystore.com).

Your Embroidery Machine

Since an embroidery machine is an investment, it's important to take time to choose the right one. Nothing helps in this process more than having a reliable local dealer who can discuss your needs and give you recommendations and advice.

If you do not sew and want a machine just for embellishing ready-made items, consider an embroidery-only machine. If you enjoy sewing and want to create your own finished projects, a machine that both sews and embroiders is your best choice. The dealer can recommend machines in a range of prices that have a variety of capabilities. Working together, you can narrow your options and select something that will be just right for you. Note: Several designs on the CD-ROM that accompanies this book require a minimum 5" × 7" (130mm × 180mm) embroidery field. Keep that in mind when selecting an embroidery machine.

Be sure to do a test run on some of the dealer's models, and never hesitate to ask questions. A good relationship with your local shop is also a great help when your machine needs a routine maintenance check or any repairs.

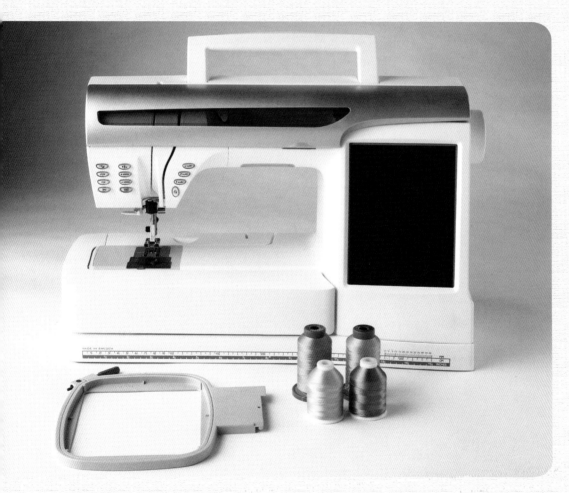

Selecting Your Embroidery Machine
There are so many models of embroidery machines available with so many features, it pays to shop around and "test drive" different manufacturers' products to find the machine that's just right for you.

Tools and Supplies

The following tools and supplies are important to have on hand as you work on the projects in this book.

CUTTING TOOLS

Scissors are an essential for all sewing projects, so invest in a good pair of shears and fine embroidery scissors. Curved scissors are invaluable for trimming stabilizer close to embroidery edges and for clipping jump threads on your finished projects. However, some sewers prefer blunt-tipped scissors for trimming stabilizer and sharp-to-the-point snips for trimming jumps.

Rotary cutters are also excellent for cutting fabric. Use them with a cutting mat and acrylic ruler.

Never use your scissors and rotary cutter on anything other than fabric and embroidery. Purchase a separate pair of scissors for cutting adhesive stabilizers as these can easily dull the blades. I've recently discovered Teflon-coated craft scissors that handle this job very well. They stay sharp and won't gum up when cutting sticky surfaces.

RULERS

Although a good straight edge ruler is sufficient, acrylic rulers used with rotary cutters, with clear measurements in a grid, are best. You'll find these in various sizes in most fabric and some craft stores.

REMOVABLE MARKING TOOLS

Water- or air-soluble markers are used not only to mark fabric but to help position the centers of randomly placed motifs, such as the fans on the *Iris & Magnolia Fans Silk Scarf* (page 22). Tailor's chalk is another temporary marking option.

Even removable marking tools should be tested first on a sample fabric scrap to make sure they don't damage the fabric. Always remove marks before ironing as heat can set the ink.

Tools for Machine Embroidery
Arranged on a cutting mat, from left to right, are ruler, fabric scisso rotary cutter, fine scissors for clipping threads, can of spray adhesi a selection of reversible marking tools.

TEMPLATES

You can use your embroidery software to print full-size templates of your design onto vellum, template paper or transparent film. These are especially useful as they allow you to see the exact size of your finished design, review its placement on your project and manipulate the templates freely as you position the designs.

FUSIBLES AND ADHESIVES

Fusible web and interfacing, spray adhesives and permanent fabric glue make finishing many of the projects in this book easier to accomplish.

Fusible fleece adds body to a tote or photo album cover. Fusible interfacing helps prevent darker mounting backgrounds such as cards or journals from showing through the fabric.

Spray adhesives are a good alternative when glue might seep through fabric or warp paper or board (see *Blue Pagoda Photo Album*, page 52).

Permanent fabric glue is ideal for attaching trims, buttons and any additional embellishments.

Be sure to use any of the spray or glue products in a room with good ventilation, and always follow the manufacturer's instructions.

STABILIZERS

Stabilizers are another important part of the machine embroidery process—they are the foundation of your finished work. While the projects presented in this book use cut-away and tear-away stabilizers, there are many types to choose from depending on your fabric choices.

Cut-away stabilizers are used for unstable fabrics that may stretch in any direction. They are left under the design to support it after the embroidery is complete (see the photo at right). To finish, trim the stabilizer close to the embroidery with a fine pair of scissors.

Tear-away stabilizers are easy to use and suitable for embroidering on stable fabrics. When your embroidery is complete, simply tear away the excess stabilizer, taking care not to pull the embroidery stitches as you go.

Water-soluble stabilizers can be completely removed with water when your embroidery is complete. Make sure that your fabric is washable and that your threads are bleed-proof before plunging them into water. To remove the water-soluble stabilizer, check the manufacturer's instructions for recommended water temperature, and rinse and soak the embroidery in plain water until all stickiness is gone.

Use water- or heat-soluble toppers on fabrics with a nap, such as terry cloth or corduroy. Because they lie on top of the fabric rather than underneath, they prevent the embroidery from sinking into the pile of the fabric.

Remember, no one stabilizer is right for every fabric. When starting out, it's a good idea to purchase a sampler pack of stabilizers so you can get the feel of how each one works on different fabrics and with various designs.

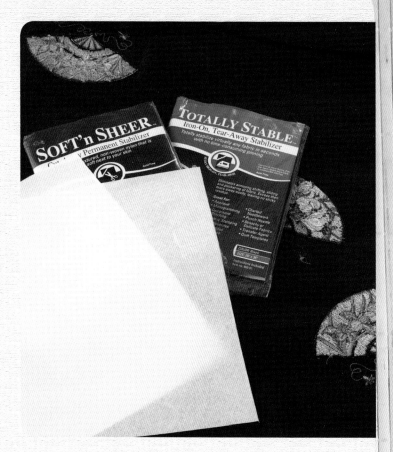

Many Types of Stabilizers for Different Uses
Consider the right stabilizer for each project. Note here the backs of the Floral Fans *after the stabilizer has been trimmed.*

Test Sew-Outs

I recommend doing a test sew-out of your design before you start on the final project. This will give you a better idea of what stabilizers will work on the fabric you've chosen; and if any of the colors don't suit you, it's easy to change your selections before embroidering the final piece. Consider this your time to play, experiment and make errors and corrections. You'll feel more confident when you begin to work on your project.

Threads and Needles

It seems the color palette of machine embroidery thread is ever expanding. What a treat to have so many delicious choices!

Machine embroidery threads are categorized by weight. I've used 40 weight thread for the designs in this book, but 50 weight threads are available in the same rainbow of colors.

Machine embroidery thread comes in many different fibers that can be combined to create interesting effects. I've used rayon and polyester threads throughout this book to reproduce the look of shimmering silks that are so often found in Asian embroidery. Polyester is especially durable and colorfast, which makes for easy care and long wear, especially for embroidery on linens and clothing. Historically, rayon's sheen has better imitated silk thread, but the newest polyester threads rival silk and rayon in appearance.

Cotton threads can provide a nice contrast with their matte finish. When using metallic threads, look for those with a polyester core that adds strength.

BOBBIN THREAD

To keep stitches smooth and to reduce bulk, use a lighter weight bobbin thread in your machine. A good rule of thumb is to use a light-colored bobbin thread on light-colored fabrics and dark bobbin thread for darker fabrics. For best results, use the type of bobbin recommended for your embroidery machine.

As your thread collection builds, you'll have endless choices for customizing individual designs to your liking.

NEEDLES

The key to a neat, clean machine-embroidered design is a good needle, one that helps maintain correct thread tension and glides through the fabric without tugging at the fibers. Routinely changing your needles (say, at the start of a new project) will help you avoid problems with breaking threads and snagging fabrics.

When choosing a needle, consider what size would work best for the fabric you're using. The larger the number, the larger the needle. A guideline is to use a 75/11 needle for lightest-weight fabrics (such as smooth silk or silk dupioni) and a heavier weight 90/14 for cottons or heavy woven fabric. Machine embroidery needles have a modified ballpoint silhouette to function on both woven and knit fabrics; they are designed to protect the thread when making closely packed embroidery stitches. There are also special needles to use for metallic threads.

Hooping Fabric

The embroidery hoop holds fabric and stabilizer in place during embroidery. It's made up of two parts: The larger outer hoop holds the tension and connects to the machine while the inner hoop secures the layers of fabric and stabilizer as you embroider.

Hooping the fabric with a good tension is necessary to prevent shifting during the embroidery process. You'll find a screw on the outside of the hoop to adjust it to the thickness and weight of your fabric and stabilizer. The designs in this book use either a 4" × 4" (100mm × 100mm) or 5" × 7" (130mm × 180mm) hoop.

HOW TO HOOP

There are various methods for hooping fabric in machine embroidery. However, hooping the fabric and stabilizer together is a good approach for many projects in this book.

1 Mark the vertical and horizontal center of the motif position with cross marks. Use a removable marking tool, such as a water-soluble pen.

2 Place the outer hoop on a flat surface and loosen the tension screw.

3 Layer the fabric and stabilizer, with fabric on top, over the outer hoop. Align the cross marks on the fabric with the vertical and horizontal centerlines on the hoop.

4 Press the inner hoop into the outer hoop, over the stabilizer and fabric. Be sure the entire inner hoop is pressed completely into the outer hoop. Tighten the thumbscrew as necessary.

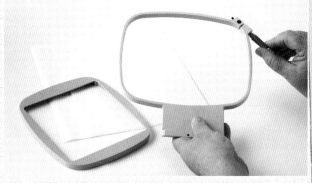

Steps 1-2
Loosen the tension screw on the outer hoop. (Although the outer hoop is being held in hand for better viewing in the photo above, it should be placed flat on the work surface for this step.)

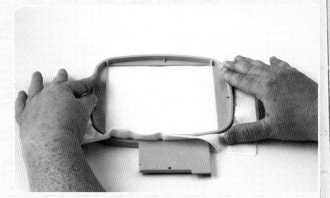

Steps 3-4
Once the fabric and stabilizer are aligned, press the inner hoop into place.

Hooping Tips

* Check the outer hoop tension and adjust the tension screw accordingly. Rehoop the fabric if necessary to make sure the tension is evenly distributed.

* Don't tug or pull at the fabric too much. Fabric that's stretched can cause the embroidery to pucker.

Embroidering on Blanks

Many of the projects included in this book are sewn on prefinished items such as pillow covers, linens and totes. There are many wonderful "blanks" available today, with items suitable for both fashion and home décor. You'll find a wide range of blanks available through manufacturers listed under *Resources* on page 126.

Embroidering large blanks such as towels or linens is a simple 1-2-3 process of stabilizing, hooping and stitching.

Sewing out such projects as the *Iris Bookmark* (page 70) takes a bit more care when stabilizing the fabric. Hoop adhesive stabilizer and remove its protective paper (or brush water-activated stabilizer with water), then attach the blank to the stabilizer. Alternatively, baste fabric or stabilizer scraps to the blank's edges, positioning the basting away from the embroidery area, to make the blank large enough to support the embroidery stitches. You will also find advice on the distributors' Web sites on how to use stabilizers on odd-shaped blanks.

Taking care with the placement of motifs such as *Bird & Blossoms* used for the *Spring Table Topper* (page 86) requires some planning, but once you are satisfied with your layout, you'll find that the embroidery goes quickly and finishing is quite simple.

Prewashing blanks before you embroider them is recommended as it allows any shrinkage to take place before you begin your embroidery.

A Variety of Blanks
Blanks are available in a range of sizes and materials, from the linen handkerchief for Poppy Handkerchief *on page 68 (above) to the fleece nightgown for* Child's Panda Nightgown *on page 48 (below). See* Resources *on page 126 for more information.*

Using the CD-ROM

The embroidery designs are ready for use on the CD-ROM tucked in the back cover of this book. You will need a computer with a CD-ROM drive to utilize the designs.

To open the designs, insert the CD-ROM into your computer. The designs are organized into different machine formats. Choose only the format specific to your machine and copy the design files onto the hard drive of your computer or directly onto a USB drive or other medium that can be read by your machine. You can also open the designs in your embroidery software, allowing further design manipulations such as rotation, mirroring and resizing (see Resizing Tip on this page for more on this option).

When the designs are successfully saved to your computer or in your embroidery software, transfer them to your embroidery machine following the manufacturer's instructions. For further details or to manage any difficulties with this process, refer to your owner's manual, consult the manufacturer's Web site for updates or call your local dealer for suggestions.

Resizing Tip

When resizing machine embroidery designs, limit the change to 10% to 20% of the design's original size. This is the usual limit automatically applied when resizing with machine controls.

For a greater change, always use resizing software that recalculates the number of stitches in the motif to keep the density consistent in the resized design.

Tips for Hand Embroidery

All of the digitized embroidery designs on the CD-ROM that accompany this book are provided in both JPG and PDF formats so that hand embroiderers can make their own embroidery transfers.

TRANSFERRING THE DESIGNS

There are several methods for creating embroidery transfers. Begin by printing a black-and-white drawing of the chosen design from the CD-ROM. Choose the method that works best with the fabric and design you're using.

Iron-on method: Use masking or painter's tape to fix the printed design face-down on a light box, or tape to a sunny window with the printed side of the paper against the glass. Trace the design with an iron-on pencil or pen (available at most needlework or craft stores), creating a mirror image of the original design. Be careful not to make any marks that you don't want transferred to the fabric.

When tracing is finished, position the printed design, transfer side down, on the right side of the fabric. Iron to transfer the design according to manufacturer's instructions.

Direct tracing method: You can trace the design directly onto light-colored lightweight fabric using a hard lead or chalk pencil or water-soluble pen. Stabilize the fabric by spraying with starch. Tape the printed design, right side up, on a light table or sunny window. Cover the printed design with fabric and trace the design lines (if working at a window, use masking or painter's tape to hold the fabric in place). Don't make any marks on the fabric that will show after the embroidery is complete in case the marks don't wash out.

Hand Embroidery Tools and Supplies
For hand embroidery, you'll need a hoop, needle, floss and small scissors.

Tracing paper method: Dressmaker's tracing paper works best for transferring designs to dark or heavy fabrics. This product is like carbon paper, with a layer of colored wax or chalk on one side.

Position the transfer paper (wax or chalk side down) on the fabric, then the printed design (printed side up). Tape the three layers in place to prevent shifting. Use a sharp tool such as a pencil or empty ballpoint pen to trace over the design lines. Check carefully as you trace to make sure the design is transferring properly to the fabric.

THREADS

Six-strand cotton embroidery floss will best recreate the look of machine embroidery. See *DMC Floss List for Hand Embroidery* (page 122) to select DMC colors for each design, or choose colors of any floss brand according to the color photographs for each project. Use two strands of floss to stitch the designs.

Many floss companies also manufacture specialty flosses in various materials and colors, including hand-dyed, overdyed and variegated in silk and rayon as well as cotton. Don't hesitate to experiment with these threads to see what kinds of effects you can achieve.

You may want to explore using silk or wool to embroider these designs as well. Stitch test swatches to see if you like the results with these threads.

HOOPS AND NEEDLES

Use a hoop when doing hand embroidery. The hoop should be big enough to allow the entire design to be worked without re-hooping. Choose a hoop that tightens securely and keeps the fabric taut in the hoop.

Use embroidery needles for hand embroidery; they have the right length, sharp points and eyes big enough for multiple strands of floss.

Butterfly 2 in Hand Embroidery
This hand-embroidered version of Butterfly 2 *was created using satin, long-short and outline stitches. Compare it to the machine-embroidered version on page 103. (Embroidery by Nancy Breen.)*

FABRICS

You can use the same fabrics for hand embroidery as for the machine embroidery projects. However, some fabrics are better suited to hand embroidery than others, so experiment with a swatch first to see if you can achieve the effect you want.

Although most embroidery floss is washable and colorfast, many fabrics may not be. Know the fabric you plan to work with and how best to care for it.

Embroidery Stitches

To recreate the appearance of the machine-embroidered designs, the hand embroidery stitches that will work best are satin stitch, long-short stitch, stem or outline stitch, straight stitch and French knot. See the photos on these two pages for illustrations of how these stitches can be used in a hand-embroidered designs. Consult a book on hand embroidery for instructions on doing these as well as other attractive stitches you might want to use.

Feel free to be creative and interpret the designs with whatever stitches will achieve the effects you desire. Experiment by stitching these designs in various embroidery styles, such as redwork or blackwork. Use as many or as few colors as you wish, and try filling in only select sections of the design, finishing the rest in outline stitch. There are many lovely approaches to creating these designs by hand.

Satin Stitch

Use satin stitch to fill in smaller areas of a design, such as the detail shapes on the butterfly's wings. Space the stitches evenly for a smooth surface. Use two strands of floss.

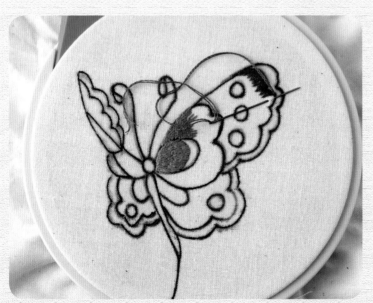

Long-Short Stitch

Use long-short stitch as a replacement for satin stitch when filling in larger areas; satin stitch can gap and become distorted when the stitches are too long.

Don't make long-short stitches too close together (this creates an uneven, lumpy surface) or too far apart (the fabric shows through the stitching and the surface loses the smooth, silky sheen.) Use two strands of floss.

Outline Stitch

Use the outline stitch *(sometimes known as the* stem stitch*) to cover solid lines, like the butterfly's attenae in the photo at left. It can also be used to outline solid areas of stitching, such as the butterfly's wings.*

Use two strands for most lines; however, one strand is best when doing finer outline work, such as the wings.

Two Geishas

The machine-embroidered geisha (above left) can be recreated in hand embroidery by using mostly satin, long-short and outline stitches. The hand-embroidered geisha (above right) shows another interpretation in hand embroidery that uses mostly outline stitch plus a few touches of satin stitch (chopsticks, ends of ribbons, facial features, white flowers on the headdress and kimono).

Note that straight stitches can be used in creative ways as alternatives to solid satin and long-short stitches (the kimono borders and collar, the hair and the ribbons). The circular motif border consists of outline stitches worked close together. French knots create the sprays of purple flowers.

CHAPTER 1

FLORAL FANS

The art of the fan played an important role in Japanese society for centuries. As individual as works of fine art, each hand-painted design was suited to a specific custom or ceremony. Using fine silks and delicate rice papers, artists found a new way to present their visions of beauty to the public. Drawing from the natural world that surrounded them, their gifted hands composed rich interpretations of sumptuous flowers, lilting birds and dreamlike landscapes.

Both men and women carried fans as accessories and in so doing made a subtle claim of class and status. I fell in love with these exquisite objects after visiting an exhibit at the Metropolitan Museum of Art many years ago. There on display were painted fans that shimmered with sprinklings of gold and silver, fans that were embellished with flowing calligraphy and fans embroidered in opulent silk threads from the Orient. Among these, the floral interpretations were my favorites. With their brilliant colors and intricate detail, they are truly precious treasures.

I've designed three floral fans: a stately iris, a splendid magnolia and a lush peony, all for you to embroider so you can adorn your own world with Asian splendor.

Iris & Magnolia Fans Silk Scarf

This shimmering silk scarf makes a lovely accessory. The iris, a symbol of faith and hope, and the magnolia, representing a love of nature, are scattered in a random pattern of fans on either end. By creating multiple templates of each fan, you can create your own arrangement to express your individual style.

MATERIALS

DESIGNS FROM CD-ROM
0101, *Iris Fan*

0102, *Magnolia Fan*

SUPPLIES & TOOLS
Silk scarf in burgundy, 16" × 36" (40.6cm × 90.1cm) (project scarf from Rubin Museum of Art, see *Resources*, page 126)

Embroidery and bobbin thread

Straight pins or painter's tape (for positioning template)

Tear-away stabilizer*

Template paper or other material

Or use adhesive stabilizer for very fragile silk; see page 14, Embroidering on Blanks, *for more about adhesive stabilizers.*

EMBROIDER THE DESIGN

1 Print the Thread and Design Guides for *Iris Fan* and *Magnolia Fan* from the CD-ROM. Transfer the designs to your embroidery machine.

2 Create templates for two *Magnolia Fans* and three *Iris Fans*. Find and mark the center of each template with cross marks.

3 Lay the scarf out full length on a flat surface. Use the diagrams on pages 24 and 25 to determine motif placement, or be creative and plan out your own pattern. Your embroidery software might allow you to mirror and rotate the fans. **Tip:** If necessary, hoop the fabric at an angle instead of rotating the motif.

Close-Up of *Iris Fan*
This fan motif is rotated 90° clockwise. See the diagram on page 24.

Close-Up of Magnolia Fan
This fan motif is rotated 90° counterclockwise. See the diagram on page 24.

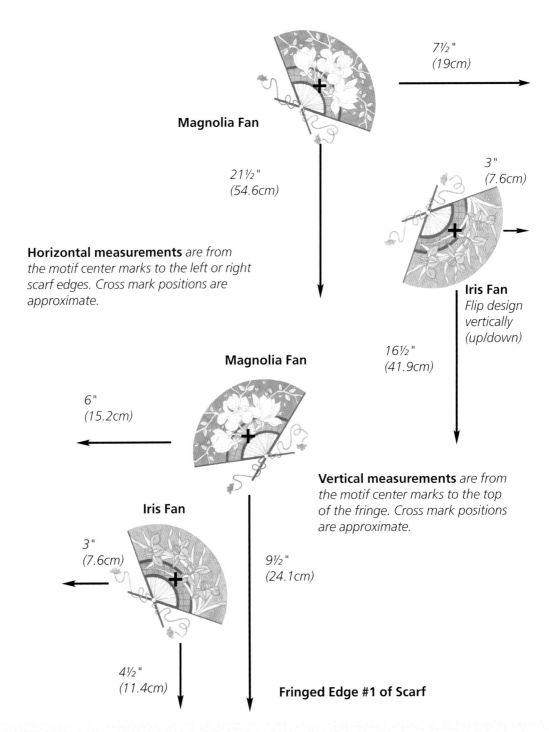

Magnolia Fan

7½ "
(19cm)

3 "
(7.6cm)

21½ "
(54.6cm)

Horizontal measurements *are from the motif center marks to the left or right scarf edges. Cross mark positions are approximate.*

Iris Fan
Flip design vertically (up/down)

16½ "
(41.9cm)

Magnolia Fan

6 "
(15.2cm)

Vertical measurements *are from the motif center marks to the top of the fringe. Cross mark positions are approximate.*

Iris Fan

3 "
(7.6cm)

9½ "
(24.1cm)

4½ "
(11.4cm)

Fringed Edge #1 of Scarf

Placement Diagram for Four of Five Fans
See page 25 for the placement diagram for the fifth fan, to be embroidered at the opposite end of the scarf.

4 For the first motif you plan to embroider, pin or tape the template into place. Hoop the scarf and stabilizer. To center each design, align the cross marks on the template with the centerlines on the hoop. Use the machine controls to position the needle over the cross marks. Remove the template before you begin stitching.

5 Embroider the design.

6 When stitching is complete, trim the jump stitches, remove the scarf from the hoop and tear away the excess stabilizer.

7 Repeat Steps 4–6 for each motif on the scarf.

Working with Silk

* Be careful with liquids around silk—moisture can cause staining.
* If you're going to wash the silk, prewash before embroidering to eliminate puckers caused by the later fabric shrinkage.
* Using templates or removable stickers to indicate embroidery placement on silk eliminates the risk that a marking tool will permanently mar the silk.
* Press using a low-temperature silk setting on your iron. Prevent scorching with a light pressing cloth laid over the finished work.

Fringed Edge #2 of Scarf

5" (12.7cm)

3" (7.6cm)

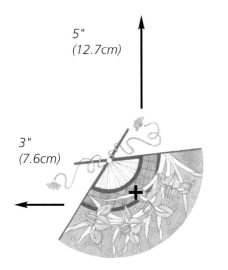

Iris Fan
Flip design vertically (up/down)

Vertical measurement
is from the motif center mark to the bottom of the fringe. Cross mark position is approximate.

Horizontal measurement
is from the motif center mark to the left scarf edge. Cross mark position is approximate.

Placement of Fifth Fan at the Opposite Fringed End
See page 24 for the placement of the first four fans.

Peony Fan Blouse

This pretty brocade blouse is just perfect to set off the lovely *Peony Fan* design. This flower, with its abundant silken petals, is one of the most revered plants in Asian culture and is a cherished symbol of prosperity. I chose three of these glorious plants for my own garden; their annual display became the inspiration for this design.

MATERIALS

DESIGN FROM CD-ROM
0103, *Peony Fan*

SUPPLIES & TOOLS
Pink brocade blouse (project blouse by Pearl River, see *Resources*, page 126)

Embroidery and bobbin threads

Cut-away mesh stabilizer

Removable marking tool

Straight pins or painter's tape (for positioning template)

Template paper or other material

Temporary spray adhesive (optional; see **Note** on page 27)

EMBROIDER THE DESIGN

1 Print the Thread and Design Guide for *Peony Fan* from the CD-ROM. Transfer the design to your embroidery machine.

2 Create a template of *Peony Fan*. Find and mark the center of the template with cross marks.

3 Lay the blouse out on a flat surface. Position the template just above the breast on the front left side of the blouse. Pin or tape the template into place. **Tip:** Try on the blouse with the template in place to check the embroidery position.

4 Hoop the blouse and stabilizer, making sure that you will be sewing through the front of the blouse only. To center the design, align the cross marks on the template with the center-lines on the hoop, even if this means the fabric grain is not aligned with the hoop sides. Use the machine controls to position the needle over the cross marks. Remove the template before you begin stitching.

   Note: If the blouse seams or trim make tradi-tional hooping impossible, use temporary adhesive spray with the cut-away stabilizer. Hoop the stabilizer alone, then spray it lightly with adhesive. Adhere the blouse to the stabilizer, aligning the template cross marks with the hoop centerlines. Remove the template before stitching.

5 Embroider the design.

6 When stitching is complete, trim the jump stitches, remove the blouse from the hoop and cut away the excess stabilizer. Cut close to the embroidery stitches, exercising caution not to clip the embroidery threads.

Close-Up of *Peony Fan*

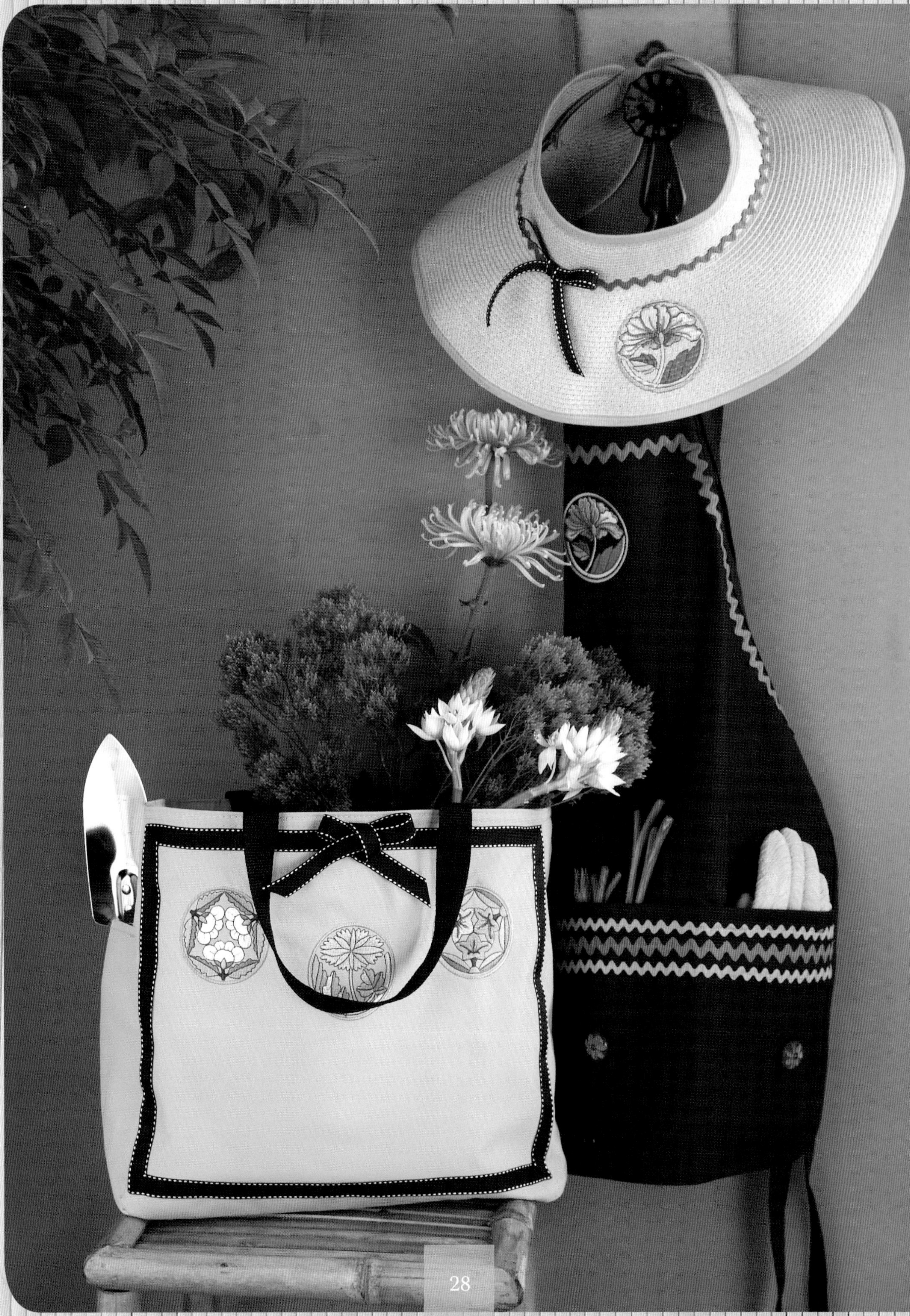

CHAPTER 2

THE JAPANESE GARDEN

To my delight, my New York City home is within walking distance of the Brooklyn Botanic Garden. Inside is a beautiful, serene Japanese garden, a welcome haven of tranquility that can carry me far beyond the noise of the city streets. When I began to think about the designs for this chapter, I was able to take a quick stroll over to a world of inspiration.

In every season, the blooming trees and brilliant flowers set the tone for the garden. Plum blossoms are the first harbingers of spring as the delicate buds celebrate rebirth and renewal. The Paulownia tree, also called the "princess tree," carries a benevolent symbol of good luck within its large purple flowers. The five-petal bellflower is the blossom of spiritual healing and is also a symbol for gratitude. The regal peony is the perfect icon for a bountiful life, while the golden chrysanthemum captures the spirit of higher wisdom.

The Japanese garden is a place of peace and tranquility. I think this may be true of every garden. There is nothing quite like an hour among the flowers to soothe the soul! Using traditional Japanese crest motifs, I've made up a lighthearted collection of projects especially for all the gardeners out there. These include a handy tote that you can dress up for a trip into town; a fun apron trimmed in bright, cheerful colors; a necessary visor to keep you protected from the sun; and a fragrant sachet bag that would make a lovely hostess gift for a fellow enthusiast.

Gardener's Sachet Bag

If you're lucky enough to have a bit of lavender in your garden, pick some to tuck into a small muslin sack. It's just the thing to fill the pocket of this pretty natural linen sachet embroidered with a circle of colorful Paulownia blossoms.

MATERIALS

DESIGN FROM CD-ROM
0203, *Paulownia Crest*

SUPPLIES & TOOLS

1 hemstitched linen cocktail napkin in oatmeal (project napkin from All About Blanks, see *Resources*, page 126)

4" × 4" (10.2cm × 10.2cm) fabric piece in complimentary color (backing)

Small lavender-filled sachet (ready-made, or sew a muslin pouch and fill with lavender)

½ yd. (45.7cm) purple satin cording

4 decorative purple satin bows, 1¾" (4.4cm) across

Embroidery and bobbin threads

Iron-on tear-away stabilizer

Needle for hand sewing

Permanent fabric glue

Removable marking tool

Sewing machine (if your embroidery machine doesn't sew)

Sewing thread (to match fabric)

EMBROIDER THE DESIGN

1 Print the Thread and Design Guide for *Paulownia Crest* from the CD-ROM. Transfer the design to your embroidery machine.

2 Fold the napkin in half horizontally and vertically to find the center. With a removable marking tool, place cross marks on the fabric at the center of the motif position.

3 Cut a piece of stabilizer large enough to fill the embroidery hoop. Lay the napkin, wrong side up, on the ironing board and cover it with the stabilizer, adhesive side down. Press to bond the stabilizer to the napkin.

4 Hoop the stabilized napkin. To center the design, align the cross marks on the napkin with the centerlines on the hoop. Use the machine controls to position the needle over the cross marks.

5 Embroider the design.

6 When stitching is complete, trim the jump stitches, remove the napkin from the hoop and tear away the excess stabilizer.

Close-Up of *Paulownia Crest*

FINISH THE PROJECT

1 Turn the raw edges of the backing fabric ¼" (6mm) to the wrong side and press.

2 With wrong sides together, center the backing fabric on the embroidered napkin. The backing's pressed edges should fall just inside the napkin hemstitches; adjust the backing if necessary.

3 Slipstitch three of the pressed edges of the backing to the napkin just inside the hemstitches to form a pocket.

4 Insert the lavender sachet or a small muslin bag filled with lavender into the pocket. Slipstitch the final edge of the backing to the napkin to close.

5 Weave satin cording in and out of the hemstitching on the coaster, beginning and ending on the back. Tie the ends together in a small bow. Use a few hand stitches or a dab of permanent fabric glue to secure the bow.

6 Use permanent fabric glue to attach a satin bow to the front of the sachet bag at each corner.

Back of *Gardener's Sachet Bag*
This shows the edges of the backing fabric slipstitched to the napkin. Note how the satin cord is woven through the hemstitching.

Gardener's Apron

Bright trims and large buttons add a perky touch to this useful apron. There are plenty of pockets to hold your gardening gear and adjustable ties for a perfect fit. Embroider the *Peony Crest* or any other design you choose and match the rickrack colors to the embroidered motif.

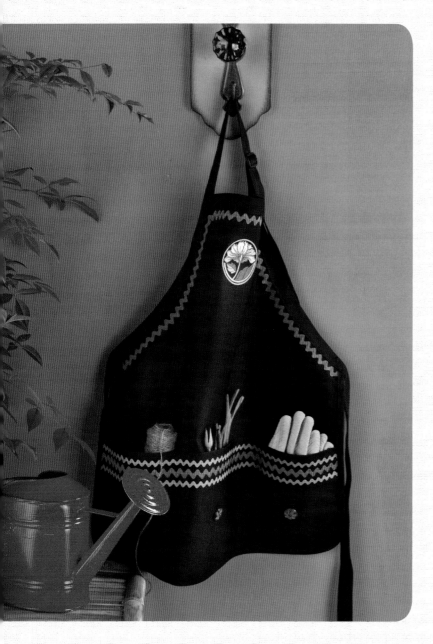

MATERIALS

DESIGN FROM CD-ROM
0204, *Peony Crest*

SUPPLIES & TOOLS

Apron, ready-made blank (3-pocket black project apron from The Sewphisticated Stitcher, see *Resources*, page 126)

45" (11.5m) pink rickrack, ½" (1.3cm) wide

45" (11.5m) lime green rickrack, ¼" (6mm) wide

3 decorative buttons (size/style/color appropriate for your apron design)

Embroidery and bobbin threads`

Adhesive tear-away stabilizer

Needle (for hand-sewing buttons)

Permanent fabric glue

Removable marking tool

Sewing thread

Straight pins or painter's tape (for positioning the template)

Template paper or other material

EMBROIDER THE DESIGN

1 Print the Thread and Design Guide for *Peony Crest* from the CD-ROM. Transfer the design to your embroidery machine.

2 Fold the apron blank in half lengthwise to find the center of the bib portion and crease. Open the apron and trace over the crease with a removable marking tool. Measure 4" (10.2cm) from the apron's upper edge and mark across the center crease to indicate the embroidery center point. **Tip:** Use tailor's chalk or a white removable marker to make the placement marks on the black apron.

3 Hoop the apron and stabilizer. To center your design, align the cross marks on the apron with the centerlines on the hoop. Use the machine controls to position the needle over the cross marks.

4 Embroider the design.

5 When stitching is complete, trim the jump stitches, remove the apron from the hoop and tear away the excess stabilizer.

EMBELLISH THE APRON

1 Glue pink rickrack aligned below the sewn edge along the upper sides and across the top of the apron, easing the rickrack into the top corners.

2 Glue alternating lime green and pink rickrack across the top of the three pockets; start by aligning the tops of the green rickrack with the stitch line. Glue a length of pink rickrack and then green rickrack ⅛" (3mm) apart. (See photo on this page.)

3 Center a button on each of the pockets and stitch into place.

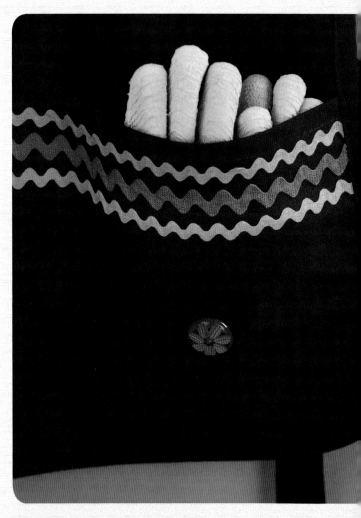

Embellishing the Apron Pockets
Although colorful rickrack and buttons are used to embellish the project apron pockets, use your creativity to explore other options. Perhaps you'd prefer buttons shaped like gardening tools or a ribbon trim. (Be sure to use the same trim on the upper part of the apron to match.)

Gardener's Visor

Don't forget to bring along sun protection when working in the garden! Embellished with *Peony Crest*, cheerful rickrack trim and a sassy bow, this clever visor rolls up and fits nicely into the pocket of your matching apron. You'll be the height of fashion sporting this pretty chapeau among the birds and bees!

MATERIALS

DESIGN FROM CD-ROM
0204, *Peony Crest*

SUPPLIES & TOOLS

Visor, ready-made (Ultra braid project visor in key lime/pink from The Sewphisticated Stitcher; see *Resources*, page 126)

25" (63.5cm) pink rickrack trim, ½" (1.3cm) wide

½ yd. (45.7cm) black and white grosgrain ribbon, ³⁄₈" (1cm) wide

Embroidery and bobbin threads

Permanent fabric glue

Removable marking tool

Straight pins or painter's tape (for positioning templates)

Tear-away stabilizer

Template paper or other material

EMBROIDER THE DESIGN

1 Print the Thread and Design Guide for *Peony Crest* from the CD-ROM. Transfer the design to your embroidery machine.

2 Create a template of *Peony Crest*. Find and mark the center of the template.

3 Fold the visor in half to find the center. Position the template at the center of the visor and 1" (2.5cm) from the bottom edge. Pin or tape the template into position.

4 Hoop the adhesive tear-away stabilizer. Remove the protective paper, exposing the sticky surface within the hoop, or brush on water to activate the adhesive.

5 Attach the visor to the hooped stabilizer. To center your design, align the cross marks on the visor with the centerlines on the hoop. Use the machine controls to position the needle over the cross marks.

6 Embroider the design.

7 When stitching is complete, trim the jump stitches, remove the visor from the hoop and cut away the excess stabilizer.

FINISH THE VISOR

1 Use the horizontal weave of the visor as a guide to glue rickrack all the way around, starting at the back and working along the natural bend of the brim.

2 Make a pretty bow from the ribbon. Glue it to the rickrack in a position that complements the embroidered crest.

Close-Up of *Peony Crest*
Note how the weave of the visor adds texture to the embroidery.

Gardener's Tote

This handy tote is easy to embroider. The added ribbon border and perky bow make it perfect for your next expedition to the garden center or flower shop. Try a placement pattern of your own to make it especially unique, and perhaps embroider additional crests on the side pockets.

MATERIALS

DESIGNS FROM CD-ROM
0201, *Bellflower Crest*

0202, *Chrysanthemum Crest*

0205, *Plum Blossom Crest*

SUPPLIES & TOOLS
Tote, ready-made, 12" × 14" × 4" (30.5cm × 35.6cm × 10.2cm) (bright lime project tote from The Sewphisticated Stitcher, see *Resources*, page 126)

Embroidery and bobbin threads

2 yds. (1.8m) black and white grosgrain ribbon, $5/8$" (1.5cm) wide

Permanent fabric glue

Removable marking tool

Tear-away stabilizer

EMBROIDER THE DESIGN

1 Print the Thread and Design Guides for the *Bellflower Crest*, *Chrysanthemum Crest* and *Plum Blossom Crest* from the CD-ROM. Transfer the designs to your embroidery machine.

2 Create a template of each crest. Find and mark the centers of each template.

3 Lay the tote out on a flat surface. Use the diagram on page 39 to determine placement, or use your creativity and plan out your own positioning. Your machine might allow you to mirror the crests, if you like. Pin or tape the templates into place.

4 Hoop the tote and stabilizer for the first motif you plan to embroider, making sure that you will be sewing through the front side of the tote only. **Tip:** Turning the tote inside out may make hooping and embroidery easier. To center the design, align the cross marks on the template with the centerlines on the hoop. Use the machine controls to position the needle over the cross marks. Remove the template before you begin stitching

5 Embroider the design.

6 When stitching is complete, trim the jump stitches, remove the tote from the hoop and tear away the excess stabilizer.

7 Repeat Steps 4–6 for the remaining templates.

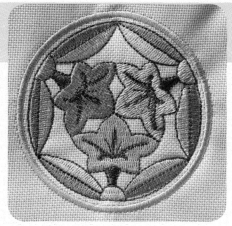

Close-Up of *Bellflower Crest*

Close-Up of *Chrysanthemum Crest*

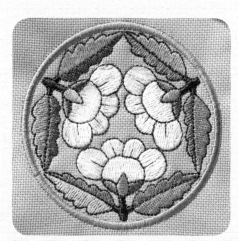

Close-Up of *Plum Blossom Crest*

FINISH THE TOTE

1 Starting and ending at the front top center of the tote, glue ribbon about ½" (1.3cm) from the top edge and the side and bottom seams. Miter the corners as you go. (See the photos on page 37 and this page.)

2 Make a pretty bow with the remaining ribbon and glue it at the center top to hide the raw ends of the ribbon.

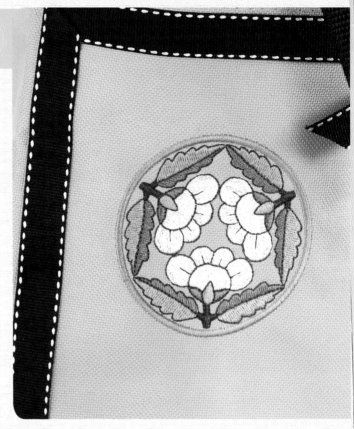

A Finished Look
Ribbon trim further enhances the appearance of this ready-made tote bag. Mitering the corners as you glue the ribbon gives the bag a professional-looking finish.

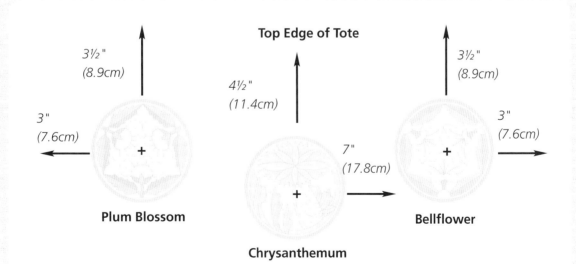

Top Edge of Tote

3½" (8.9cm)

4½" (11.4cm)

3" (7.6cm)

3½" (8.9cm)

3" (7.6cm)

7" (17.8cm)

Plum Blossom

Chrysanthemum

Bellflower

Placement Diagram for *Gardener's Tote*
Measurements are from the motif center marks to the top and side edges of the tote front. Positions of cross marks are approximate.

CHAPTER 3

PLAYFUL PANDAS

Pandas enjoy a mystical reputation in China. These treasured animals were thought to protect the Emperor and his family from natural disaster and to ward off evil spirits. Today, pandas are an endangered species and protected themselves. They live on the mountainous slopes of China, feasting in shady groves teeming with their favorite food, bamboo.

The images of pandas in the wild capture our hearts, so I thought they would be perfect for a set of projects for children (or the child in you). I've designed five different poses of these cuddly friends with a border worked in simple outline stitch. I also created a traditional *Double Happiness* motif to intersperse through your design layouts.

Embroider a cozy afghan using all five pandas. Your machine might allow you to flip the poses and create a lot of variation. Choose your four favorite pandas for a matching pillow top. For your special little one, embroider one of the motifs on a pretty fleece nightgown or a set of boy's pajamas. These designs would also work well on sweatshirts, kids' backpacks, craft aprons and just about anything that you can embroider.

Cozy Pandas Afghan

The *Double Happiness* motif adds an extra smile for whoever snuggles up with this cozy afghan. By using a fabric with bordered squares already woven in, you can stitch and display the many sides of these adorable pandas.

MATERIALS

DESIGNS FROM CD-ROM
0301, *Panda 1*

0302, *Panda 2*

0303, *Panda 3*

0304, *Panda 4*

0305, *Panda 5*

0306, *Double Happiness Symbol*

SUPPLIES & TOOLS
1 Anne cloth afghan (project afghan cloth by Zweigart, see *Resources*, page 126)

Embroidery and bobbin threads

Iron-on cut-away mesh stabilizer

Removable marking tool

Sewing machine (if your embroidery machine doesn't sew)

Sewing thread (color to match afghan)

PREPARE THE FABRIC

1 Before you begin the embroidery, trim the afghan to measure 5 squares wide by 7 squares high, leaving 2 " (5.1cm) of fabric beyond the raised border.

2 Using white sewing thread, create a fringe around the afghan by running a machine stitch ¾ " (19mm) beyond the raised border on all four sides.

3 Trim the afghan 1 " (25mm) beyond the running stitch and remove the weave to the stitching line.

EMBROIDER THE DESIGN

1 Print the Thread and Design Guides for *Pandas 1, 2, 3, 4* and *5* and *Double Happiness Symbol* from the CD-ROM. Transfer the designs to your embroidery machine.

2 Lay the afghan out on a flat surface. Find the center of each woven square that you plan to embroider using the diagram on page 44 as a guide. With a removable marking tool, place cross marks on the fabric at the center of each square.

3 Iron a piece of cut-away stabilizer to the wrong side of the first square to be embroidered. Hoop the afghan and stabilizer, aligning the cross marks with the centerlines on the hoop. Use the machine controls to position the needle over the cross marks.

4 Embroider the design.

5 When stitching is complete, trim the jump stitches, remove the afghan from the hoop and cut away the excess stabilizer.

6 Repeat Steps 3–5 for each motif, stabilizing and re-hooping the fabric for each.

Close-Up of *Panda 3*

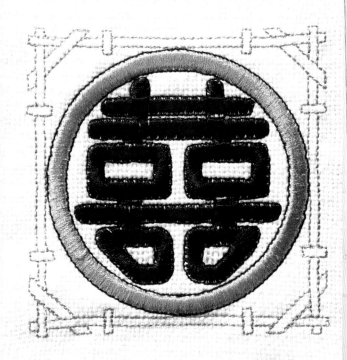

Close-Up of *Double Happiness Symbol*
Repeat the Double Happiness *motif five times on the afghan; follow the placement as indicted on the diagram on page 44.*

Double Happiness Symbol		Panda 1 Reversed		Double Happiness Symbol
	Panda 2 Reversed		Panda 3	
Panda 3 Reversed		Panda 5 Reversed		Panda 1
	Panda 4	Double Happiness Symbol	Panda 4 Reversed	
Panda 1 Reversed		Panda 5		Panda 2
	Panda 2 Reversed		Panda 1	
Double Happiness Symbol		Panda 3		Double Happiness Symbol

Placement Diagram for *Cozy Panda Afghan*
In the above diagram, "reversed" indicates the mirror image of the original design.

Pandas Pillow

Embroider a darling panda pillow to go along with your afghan. A pretty grosgrain ruffle around the edge adds a colorful splash to the embroidery's simple palette. To make the project more suited to a boy, try using a simple braided trim in gold or black instead of the ruffle.

MATERIALS

DESIGNS FROM CD-ROM
0301, *Panda 1*

0302, *Panda 2*

0303, *Panda 3*

0304, *Panda 4*

SUPPLIES & TOOLS
2' × 2' (61cm × 61cm) square piece of Anne cloth (from leftover fabric from *Cozy Panda Afghan*, page 42)

½ yd. (45.7cm) fabric in complimentary color (for backing)

2 yds. (1.8m) ruffled grosgrain trim, 2–3" (5.1cm × 7.6cm) wide (green to match the bamboo leaves, or a color you find pleasing)

1 decorative button (to match ruffle, or color/size as desired)

One 14" × 14" (35.6cm × 35.6cm) square pillow form

Embroidery and bobbin threads

Iron-on cut-away stabilizer

Removable marking tool

Sewing machine (if your embroidery machine doesn't sew)

Sewing thread (color to match pillow)

PREPARE THE FABRIC

Before you begin the embroidery, trim the Anne cloth to a four-square section, leaving 2" (5.1cm) of fabric beyond the outer raised border.

EMBROIDER THE DESIGN

1 Print the Thread and Design Guides for *Pandas 1*, *2*, *3* and *4* from the CD-ROM. Transfer the designs to your embroidery machine.

2 Lay the Anne cloth square on a flat surface. Find the center of each square to be embroidered. With a removable marking tool, place cross marks on the fabric at the center of each square.

3 Iron a piece of cut-away stabilizer to the wrong side of the first square to be embroidered. Hoop the fabric and stabilizer, aligning the cross marks with the centerlines on the hoop. Use the machine controls to position the needle over the cross marks.

4 Embroider the design.

5 When stitching is complete, trim the jump stitches, remove the pillow top from the hoop and cut away the excess stabilizer.

6 Repeat Steps 3–5 for each motif, stabilizing and re-hooping the fabric for each.

Close-Up of *Panda 2* Reversed (above top) and *Panda 4* Reversed (above bottom)

Panda 2 Reversed	Panda 4 Reversed
Panda 3 Reversed	Panda 1

***Panda Pillow* Placement Diagram**

FINISHING THE PILLOW

1 Beginning at the center bottom with right sides facing, match the gathered edge of the trim to the raw edge of the embroidered Anne cloth. Baste the trim into place all the way around the pillow top, folding in extra fullness at the corners.

2 Cut two 13" × 15" (33cm × 38.1cm) pieces of backing fabric.

3 On each piece of backing fabric, turn one long (15"/38.1cm) edge under ¼" (6mm), then turn under ¼" (6mm) again and stitch.

4 Place the embroidered pillow top face up on a flat surface. Position one piece of backing fabric over the pillow top, right sides together, with raw edges matching and the basted trim in between. The stitched long edge of the backing should be toward the center.

Place the second piece of backing fabric face down so its stitched long edge overlaps the stitched edge of the first backing fabric piece at the center of the pillow. Match raw edges with the embroidered pillow top, with the basted trim in between

5 Sew around all four edges using a ½" (1.3cm) seam.

Close-Up of *Panda 3* **Reversed (above top) and** *Panda 1* **(above bottom)**

6 Turn the pillow cover to the right side through the opening formed by the overlapping backing fabric in the center of the pillow. Sew a decorative button to the front center of the pillow cover.

7 Insert the pillow form through the opening in the center back of the pillow.

Child's Panda Nightgown

Soft fleece is just right for this darling nightgown. When you embroider the design, omit the gold border that surrounds the motifs in the other panda projects in this chapter. For boys' pajamas, try placing the embroidery on a patch pocket or at the top center of a tee.

MATERIALS

DESIGN FROM CD-ROM
0305, *Panda 5*

SUPPLIES & TOOLS
1 child's white fleece nightgown, ready-made (project nightgown from Land's End, see *Resources*, page 126)

Embroidery and bobbin threads

Cut-away stabilizer

Removable marking tool

Straight pins or painter's tape (for positioning templates)

Template paper or other material

Temporary spray adhesive

Water-soluble topping

EMBROIDER THE DESIGN

1 Print the Thread and Design Guide for *Panda 5* from the CD-ROM. Transfer the design to your embroidery machine.

2 To plan your design placement, make a template of *Panda 5*. Find and mark the center of the template.

3 Lay the nightgown out on a flat surface. With spray adhesive, secure water-soluble topping to the surface of the gown over the embroidery area. Pin or tape the template over the water-soluble topper on the upper left front of the nightgown (shown just to the left of the button placket on the project gown).

4 Hoop the gown, stabilizer and topping, making sure that you will be sewing through the front of the gown only. To position the design, align the cross marks on the template with the centerlines on the hoop. Use the machine controls to position the needle over the cross marks. Remove the template before you begin stitching.

5 To eliminate the gold border on the motif, use the machine's controls to skip forward past color one. Embroider the remainder of the design.

6 When stitching is complete, trim the jump stitches and remove the gown from the hoop. Gently tear or cut away as much water-soluble topper as possible. Follow the manufacturer's instructions to remove the remaining water-soluble topper.

Close-Up of *Panda 5*
Note placement of motif in relation to the collar and button placket.

PAGODA & GEISHA

The lush scenery and stately pagoda of the classic blue willow pattern inspired my *Blue Pagoda Photo Album* (page 52). The willow china pattern, in which rich royal blue in all of its subtle variations works with the light and shadow of the exotic landscapes, was first introduced in England in the late 18th century. As trade with the Far East blossomed, all things Asian became more popular and were in high demand among the privileged classes, such as the fashionable Chinoiserie. Into the late 19th century, Japonisme was the style of the day and greatly influenced the Art Nouveau movement.

The exquisite geisha of *ukiyo-e* (Japanese woodblock prints) are recreated in my *Asian Beauty Hand Mirror* (page 55). Literally meaning "pictures of the floating world," ukiyo-e reflected a life that was lived for the moment, drifting in and out with the latest fashions. Print makers chose the most beautiful and intelligent geisha as their models. Geisha were highly trained in music, poetry and the Japanese tea ceremony. Their dress and make-up were an art in themselves, often taking hours of preparation. The careful layering of clothing and the painting of delicate features took on their own ritual and symbolism.

Enjoy creating these individual expressions of Asian beauty.

Blue Pagoda Photo Album

Remember a wonderful holiday or travel adventure by filling this handsome keepsake album with your favorite photos. It also makes a special bon voyage gift for a dear friend. Choose a coordinating fabric and some pretty trim to match your embroidery. Making up this covered binder is easy with the instructions I've provided.

MATERIALS

DESIGN FROM CD-ROM
0401, *Blue Pagoda*

SUPPLIES & TOOLS

9" × 9" (22.9cm x 22.9cm) piece of white Monaco evenweave (#MO-0236-6750 from Charles Craft, see *Resources*, page 126)

¼ yd. (.25m) blue fabric (outside cover)

¼ yd. (.25m) violet fabric (inside cover)

¼ yd. (.25m) iron-on interfacing, medium weight

¼ yd. (.25m) cotton batting

1 small 3-ring binder photo album 6"w × 7"h (15.2cm × 17.8cm)

1 yd. (1m) of blue ribbon, ³⁄₈" (1.5cm) wide

1 decorative button (size and style appropriate for cover)

Two 6" × 7" (15.2cm × 17.8cm) pieces of heavy card

Embroidery and bobbin threads

Iron

Permanent fabric glue

Removable marking tool

Spray adhesive

Tear-away stabilizer

EMBROIDER THE DESIGN

1 Print the Thread and Design Guide for *Blue Pagoda* from the CD-ROM. Transfer the design to your embroidery machine.

2 Cut a piece of iron-on interfacing slightly smaller than the fabric square. Lay the evenweave fabric face down on the ironing board and make sure the grainlines are straight and perpendicular to each other. Following manufacturer's instructions, fuse the interfacing to the fabric wrong side.

3 Hoop the fabric and stabilizer, keeping the evenweave grainlines straight in the hoop.

4 Embroider the design.

5 When stitching is complete, trim the jump stitches, remove the fabric from the hoop and tear away the excess stabilizer.

Close-Up of *Blue Pagoda*

FINISH THE PHOTO ALBUM

1 Trim the embroidered fabric to 4½" (11.4cm) square, keeping the design centered.

2 Lay the photo album binder open flat on the batting. Trace the outer dimensions of the album onto the batting. Cut the batting 1" (25mm) outside the traced lines all around.

3 Working in a well-ventilated area, spray the outside front album cover with adhesive. Attach the batting, then repeat for the spine and back cover. Don't pull the batting over the cover too tightly, and make sure the album can close correctly. Trim the batting flush with the edges of the album cover.

4 Lay the open album flat on the outer cover fabric. Mark 2" (5.1cm) from all four edges and cut the fabric. From the same fabric, cut two strips the length of the album's metal spine and 3" (7.6cm) wide. Turn one long edge of each strip ¼" (6mm) to the wrong side and press. Spray adhesive on the back of each strip and slide the folded edge under each side of the metal spine.

5 Cut two 8" × 9" (20.3cm × 22.9cm) pieces of inside cover fabric. Spray adhesive on one side of each piece of cut card. Center each card, adhesive side down, on the wrong side of a piece of inside cover fabric. Turn the edges of the fabric to the back of each card and fix with permanent glue.

6 Center the open album on the outside cover fabric. Starting at the center of each edge, leaving the corners and 3" (7.6cm) from the spine free, turn all fabric edges to the inside of the album's covers and glue. Next, ease the corners of the fabric over the covers to fit, then glue.

7 On both sides of the spine at the top and bottom, measure the fabric ½" (1.3cm) from the cover's hinge fold to the fabric's outer edge, then clip to within ½" (1.3cm) of the edge of the album. Fold the top fabric tab created by the two straight cuts and tuck it behind the top edge of the metal spine; glue into place. Repeat for the bottom of the spine.

8 Apply glue along the edges of the back of each covered card. Center a card, glue side down, over each inside cover of the album, making sure the cover fold along the spine is free so the cover can close. Press the card firmly into place. Cover with a weight and allow to dry completely.

Inside Cover of *Blue Pagoda Photo Album*
Make sure the covered card on the inside cover doesn't interfere with the hinge near the spine, otherwise the album won't close properly. Note how the strips of fabric have been inserted under the metal spine.

9 Center the embroidery on the cover and glue into place, taking care that no glue oozes out.

10 Starting and ending at the center bottom of the embroidered piece, draw a thin bead of fabric glue around the edges and cover with ribbon, mitering the corners as you go. Glue a decorative button where the ends of the ribbon meet.

Asian Beauty Hand Mirror

In luxurious silk and hand-embroidered kimonos, the geisha entertained their guests and became the ultimate expression of femininity and grace. The enticing spirit of the geisha invites you to reflect on your own beauty with this elegant hand mirror, embroidered in rich colors on delicate silk.

MATERIALS

DESIGN FROM CD-ROM
0402, *Geisha*

SUPPLIES & TOOLS
9" × 9" (22.9cm × 22.9cm) square of pale green dupioni silk

½ yd. (45.7cm) decorative trim, such as narrow braid, in a complimentary color

1 decorative button (style/size appropriate for design; project mirror uses a carved wooden button)

Cotton batting

3 small lilac crystals

2 small pink crystal flowers

1 large wooden hand mirror (#23301 from Sudberry House, see *Resources*, page 126)

Embroidery and bobbin threads

Gem glue (optional)

Permanent fabric glue

Tear-away stabilizer

EMBROIDER THE DESIGN

1 Print the Thread and Design Guide for *Geisha* from the CD-ROM. Transfer the design to your embroidery machine.

2 Hoop the fabric and stabilizer, keeping the fabric grain straight in the hoop.

3 Embroider the design.

4 When stitching is complete, trim the jump stitches, remove the silk from the hoop and cut away the excess stabilizer.

Close-Up of *Geisha*
Note the positioning of the crystals and crystal flowers.

FINISH THE HAND MIRROR

1 Using the mounting board included with the mirror as a template, cut a piece of cotton batting to the same size. Layer the embroidery over the batting, then position both on the mounting board. Mount the embroidery according to the manufacturer's instructions that accompany the mirror.

2 Starting and ending at center bottom, use permanent fabric glue to attach decorative trim around the mounted embroidery, covering the edge. Attach a decorative button where the ends of the trim meet.

3 Attach the crystal flowers at the bottom of the headpiece and the small crystals at the flower tips with gem glue or permanent fabric glue. Use the photo on page 56 as a reference.

Crystals: Glue or Heat Set?

Although heat-set (or hot fix) crystals and gems are popular and easy to use, consider glue instead to attach the crystals and flowers to the mirror. A slip-up with a heat set tool or hot crystal could ruin the silk dupioni or your embroidery.

Be careful with glues as well—they can stain fabric. Some experts believe that gem glue creates a better bond than permanent fabric glue, and the bond may be more durable.

Heat-set crystals can be used, unheated, with gem or fabric glue. In fact, some experts say the texture of the adhesive coating on the back of heat-set crystals "grabs" the gem or fabric glue and creates a better bond.

CHAPTER 5

FOUR SEASONS KIMONOS

Art became fashion at the height of the Edo period in Japan. With the people's increased wealth and demand for more luxurious fabrics, the humble woven kimono became the ultimate expression of feminine guile and beauty. Combining the most luxurious silk threads and the finest embroidery, these works of art spoke volumes about the women who wore them. The more affluent the wearer, the more elaborate the costume. It's amazing to get up close to these works of art now and see the intricate handwork that has gone into their making.

Layers and layers of jewel-toned threads depict all forms of birds and flowers, symbols and landscapes. These lavish garments were created as an ideal balance of art and design. Today they are reserved for special occasions such as weddings and birthdays. Drawing inspiration from these symbols of Japanese culture, I've designed four different floral kimonos to celebrate the changing seasons. Two of those designs are presented in projects in this chapter. A bright-eyed clematis heralds the summer season on an easy-to-make cover to protect your daily journal. A special mahogany keepsake box frames a springtime kimono decorated with flowing wisteria and bountiful peonies. Two additional designs are included on the CD-ROM: an autumn kimono decorated with the noble chrysanthemum set against a background the color of golden autumn leaves, and a winter kimono with a dark blue field to set off the sparkling white of the delicate plum blossoms that start the never-ending cycle all over again.

All four kimonos are suitable for many other applications. Try embroidering these designs on a silky kimono wrap of your own or make them up into a wall hanging to display in your home.

Summer Kimono Journal Cover

As you keep your summer journal close at hand, protect it beautifully with this easy-to-make cover. Choose bright fabrics for your project to go along with the sunny season. The yin/yang symbol at the top of the kimono reflects peace and harmony. It brings to mind a cool spot beneath a bower of cheerful clematis, whose twining stems are a sign of cherished affection.

MATERIALS

DESIGN FROM CD-ROM
0501, *Summer Kimono*

SUPPLIES & TOOLS
One 12" × 12" (30.5cm × 30.5cm) piece gold fabric (for embroidered panel)

One 6" × 8" (15.2cm × 20.3cm) piece paper-backed fusible web

½ yd. (45.7cm) mauve fabric (for cover)

¼ yd. (20.3cm) iron-on interfacing, medium weight

¼ yd. (20.3cm) fusible fleece

1 yd. (91.4cm) black velvet ribbon, ¼" (6mm) wide

1 decorative button (size/style appropriate for cover design)

4 decorative beads (for ribbon)

1 softbound blank journal, 6" × 8" (15.2cm × 20.3cm)

Embroidery and bobbin threads

Iron

Needle for hand-sewing tacking stitches (optional)

Permanent fabric glue

Removable marking tool

Sewing machine (if your embroidery machine doeesn't sew)

Sewing thread (color to match fabric)

Straight pins or painter's tape

Tear-away stabilizer

EMBROIDER THE DESIGN

1 Print the Thread and Design Guide for *Summer Kimono* from the CD-ROM. Transfer the design to your embroidery machine.

2 Cut a piece of iron-on interfacing slightly smaller than the fabric square. Lay the fabric face down on the ironing board and fuse the interfacing to the fabric wrong side, following the manufacturer's instructions.

3 Hoop the interfaced fabric and stabilizer.

4 Embroider the design.

5 When stitching is complete, trim the jump stitches, remove the fabric from the hoop and tear away the excess stabilizer.

FINISH THE JOURNAL

1 Trim the embroidered fabric to measure 4½" (11.4 cm) wide and 5½" (14 cm) high, keeping the design centered.

2 Place the journal, opened flat, on top of the cover fabric. Measure 4½" (11.4cm) from the edges of the journal all around and cut the fabric. Fold ¼" (6mm) to the wrong side of the fabric and machine- or hand-stitch into place.

3 With the journal centered on the fabric, fold the top and bottom edges of the fabric to meet the top and bottom edges of the journal. Remove the journal and press the folds into place.

Close-Up of *Summer Kimono*
Black velvet ribbon creates a lovely frame for this piece.

4 Reposition the opened journal and fold the side edges of the fabric over the front and back covers, creating pockets. Close the journal to make sure there's enough "give" in the fabric for a proper fit; adjust the pockets as needed. Remove the journal and press the pocket folds into place.

5 Place the folded cover fabric on the fusible fleece and mark the cover dimensions. Remove the cover and trim the fleece just inside the marks. Center the fleece, adhesive side down, within the folded cover fabric. Press to fuse according to manufacturer's instructions. Use small strips of fusible web to secure the undersides of the side pockets, top and bottom. Iron to fuse. (Fix the pockets in place with small tacking stitches, if you prefer.)

6 Cut a piece of fusible web the same size as the embroidered rectangle. Follow manufacturer's instructions to fuse the web to the embroidered rectangle's wrong side. Allow to cool, then remove the protective paper. Slip the journal into the fabric cover, with the journal's original covers inserted into the fabric pockets. Center the embroidered panel, right side up, on the journal front. Pin or tape into place, then remove the journal cover.

7 Lay the journal cover face up on an ironing board, remove the pins or tape and double check the position of the panel. Cover with a press cloth to protect the embroidery, then press to fuse the embroidery to the cover.

8 Beginning and ending at the center bottom of the embroidered panel, glue velvet ribbon over the outer edge of the embroidery, mitering the corners as you go. Trim the excess ribbon so the two ends meet. Glue a decorative button over the join.

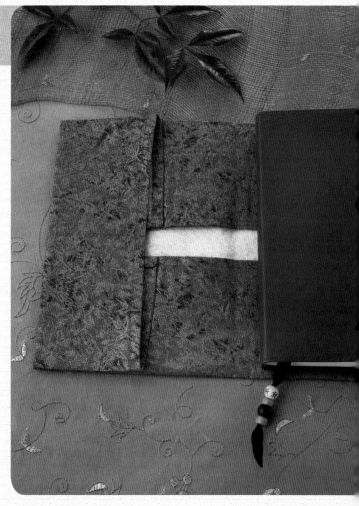

Cover Is Removable
Using a softbound journal with flexible covers makes it easier to slip them in and out of the fabric pockets. It also means you can use the embroidered cover on a new journal when the old one gets filled.

9 Glue one end of the remaining length of ribbon within the top of the journal's spine (some journals will have a gap when the journal is open) or to the inner back cover near the top of the spine. String a few decorative beads on the ribbon; put a touch of glue within the top and bottom beads to hold them in place. Trim the ribbon to the desired length.

Spring Kimono Keepsake Box

This *Spring Kimono* design has the precious qualities of a fine miniature painting. Mount it in an elegant keepsake box to create a treasured gift for a friend or loved one, or present it to a happy bride.

MATERIALS

DESIGN FROM CD-ROM
0502, *Spring Kimono*

SUPPLIES & TOOLS

12" × 12" (30cm × 30cm) gold silk dupioni

12" × 12" (30cm x 30cm) cotton batting

24" (61cm) decorative black cord

1 decorative button (style/size appropriate for project design)

Wooden keepsake box about 8½" x 7" × 3" (21.6cm × 17.8cm × 7.6cm) with a 5" × 7" (12.7cm ×17.8cm) design space in lid (project shows Large Presentation Box #99941 by Sudberry House, see *Resources*, page 126)

Embroidery and bobbin threads

Double-sided tape

Permanent fabric glue

Tear-away stabilizer

EMBROIDER THE DESIGN

1 Print the Thread and Design Guide for *Spring Kimono* from the CD-ROM. Transfer the design to your embroidery machine.

2 Hoop the fabric and stabilizer, roughly centering the hoop on the fabric.

3 Embroider the design.

4 Trim the jump stitches, remove the fabric from the hoop and tear away the excess stabilizer.

Close-Up of *Spring Kimono*

Keepsake Box: Alternative Techniques

You can embroider any design on this book's CD-ROM and use the technique described on page 65 to create a keepsake box.

However, maybe you would prefer to use a different type of box: a paper maché or craft wood box that you've finished yourself, a vintage container or any kind of box that doesn't have an opening in the lid for an insert.

You can follow the instructions for *Finish the Photo Album* on pages 53–54, gluing the embroidered panel to a box lid instead of an album cover.

If you use a box with a lid opening that does not include a mounting board, cut a board to fit from masonite, foam board or heavy cardboard (choose your material according to the depth of the recessed area). For a backing board, cover a piece of cardstock with a complimentary fabric, felt or decorative paper. Glue the backing board over the insert, the right side of the board facing the box interior.

FINISH THE KEEPSAKE BOX

1 Use the mounting board that comes with the box as a template to cut a piece of cotton batting. Trim the embroidered fabric 1" (25mm) larger on each side than the mounting board. Center the embroidered fabric right side up over the batting and position both on the mounting board. Wrap the raw edges of the fabric to the back of the mounting board and adhere with double-stick tape, folding in the fullness at each corner.

2 Insert the mounted embroidery into the box lid from the inside. Put a bit of glue on the edges of the wrong side of the backing board that comes with the box and lay the backing board over the wrong side of the mounted embroidery. The right side of the backing board should be showing inside the box once the insert is in place. (Some premade boxes come with swivels to secure the insert and backing board. For those, no gluing is necessary.)

3 On the right side of the lid, glue black cord around the edge of the insert, starting at the center bottom within the recessed area of the front lid. Trim the ends flush with each other and add a decorative button where the ends of the cord meet.

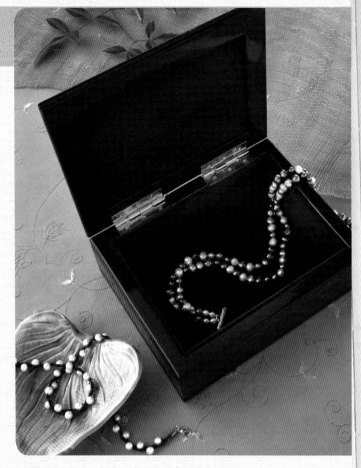

A Finished Look for the Inside of the Box
This kind of box comes with a backing board covered with the same material that was used to line the box. This creates a clean, finished look that complements the outside appearance. See Keepsake Box: Alternative Techniques *on page 64 if you're using a box that doesn't have either a mounting board or backing board.*

CHAPTER 6

NATURE'S BEAUTY

Nature is an integral part of life in Asian culture. From the ancient practice of *feng shui* we learn that the life force, or *ch'i*, must flow easily between our natural and man-made environments in order to have a balanced life. By bringing the glory of nature into our homes, we coexist with her and so invite happiness, health and prosperity to our lives.

The Oriental Poppy suggests a foreign and exotic world. With its delicate, silky petals in flaming red, this flower represents a forceful, creative energy—an important symbol of new life in the art and practice of *feng shui*. To come upon a hillside filled with their burst of color swaying in the wind is a treat for the senses.

The exotic orchid is one of nature's finest gifts. This flower captures the imagination with mysterious beauty and is one of the four noble plants of China, often given as a token of friendship and love.

The Siberian Iris grows along brooks and streams, framing the water's edge in velvety purple. I let these spring beauties grow freely along the creek in my country garden. Its sword-like foliage is said to cut through stagnant *ch'i* and bring an even flow of energy to the earth around it.

The wonderfully subtle hues of changing autumn leaves are among nature's most extraordinary visual gifts. The delicate leaves of the Japanese maple put on a brilliant display every year. In various shades of rust, red and copper, they light up the landscape one last time before fading quietly into the early winter chill.

The *Oriental Poppy* and *Japanese Maple Leaf* motifs look clean and crisp on prefinished linen accessories. I've provided three versions of each so you can mix and turn them as you like to create some beautiful pieces for your home. I designed a journal and bookmark with the *Orchid* and *Iris* respectively for quiet moments when you want to reflect, make notes on a day well spent or curl up with your favorite book.

Poppy Handkerchief

Pretty poppies make a sweet hostess gift when embroidered on a delicate handkerchief. Use your creative spirit to make up your own arrangements of the three motifs. Try them on embroidered bed linens, a cheerful tote or any number of prefinished items.

MATERIALS

DESIGNS FROM CD-ROM
0601, *Oriental Poppy 1*,
0602, *Oriental Poppy 2* or
0603, *Oriental Poppy 3**

*project uses *Oriental Poppy 3*

SUPPLIES & TOOLS
1 white eyelet-edged linen handkerchief (the project handkerchief is the mosaic stitch hankie, 16" [40.6cm] square, from All About Blanks, see *Resources*, page 126)

1 yd. (91.4cm) narrow red ribbon, ⅛" (3mm) wide (or a width that fits through the eyelets of your handkerchief)

Embroidery and bobbin threads

Adhesive tear-away stabilizer

Large-eyed needle or a bodkin narrow enough to fit through the eyelets (for weaving ribbon)

Removable marking tool

EMBROIDER THE DESIGN

1 Print the Thread and Design Guide for the *Oriental Poppy* design of your choice from the CD-ROM. Transfer the design to your embroidery machine.

2 Fold the handkerchief in half diagonally to determine the center of one corner. With a removable marking tool, place cross marks along the corner fold and 2" (5.1cm) up from the corner of the fabric (excluding the edging).

3 Hoop the stabilizer and activate or expose the adhesive. Adhere the handkerchief to the stabilizer, orienting the handkerchief diagonally and aligning the cross marks on the corner of the handkerchief with the centerlines on the hoop. Use the machine controls to position the needle over the cross marks. Remember that the design should be positioned so the bottom, not the top, of the motif is nearest the trim.

4 Embroider the design.

5 When stitching is complete, trim the jump stitches, remove the embroidery from the hoop and tear away the excess stabilizer.

FINISH THE HANDKERCHIEF

1 Thread a large-eyed needle or bodkin of appropriate size with red ribbon. Beginning in the corner below the embroidered design, weave the ribbon in and out of the eyelet edge of the handkerchief. Leave a tail of ribbon long enough to tie a bow.

2 Bring the needle or bodkin through the same eyelet where you began. Remove the ribbon from the needle or bodkin and adjust the ends to make them even, if necessary. Tie a small bow. Trim the ribbon ends if they're too long.

Close-up of *Oriental Poppy 3*

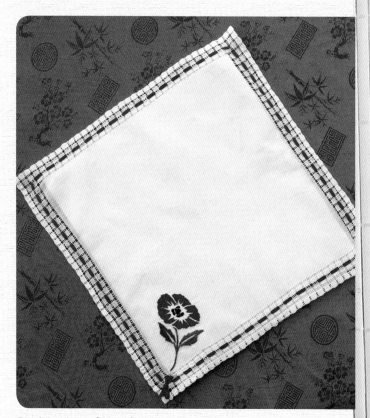

Positioning of Motif on Handkerchief

Iris Bookmark

The beauty of my early spring garden is always a sight to behold, especially when the irises begin to bloom. A sea of blue flags graces the banks of the brook behind the house, standing tall and proud. A Chinese symbol of positive energy, the regal iris is said to bring a smooth flow of life force to the garden.

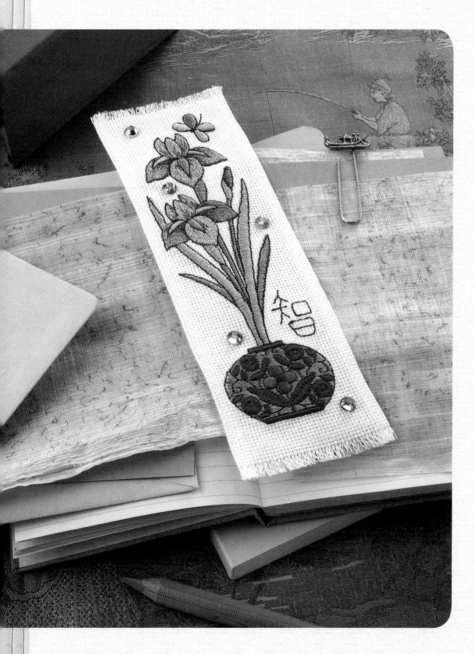

MATERIALS

DESIGN FROM CD-ROM
0604, *Iris*

SUPPLIES & TOOLS
2½" × 8" (6.4cm × 20.3cm) 18 count white Aida bookmark (project bookmark #BO-0790-6750-EA by Charles Craft, see *Resources*, page 126)

2½" × 8" (6.4cm × 20.3cm) piece white felt for backing

2½" × 8" (6.4cm × 20.3cm) paper-backed fusible web

5 small lilac crystals

Embroidery and bobbin threads

Cut-away stabilizer

Iron

Permanent fabric glue

Removable marking tool

Temporary spray adhesive

EMBROIDER THE DESIGN

1 Print the Thread and Design Guide for *Iris* from the CD-ROM. Transfer the design to your embroidery machine.

2 Fold the ready-made bookmark in half horizontally and vertically to determine the center. With a removable marking tool, place cross marks on the fabric at the center of the motif position.

3 Hoop the stabilizer and spray it lightly with temporary adhesive. Adhere the bookmark to the stabilizer, aligning the cross marks on the bookmark with the centering marks on the hoop. Use the machine controls to position the needle over the cross marks.

4 Embroider the design.

5 When stitching is complete, trim the jump stitches, remove the bookmark from the hoop and cut away the excess stabilizer.

FINISH THE BOOKMARK

1 Position five lilac crystals as you like on the bookmark and attach with permanent fabric glue. (See *Crystals: Glue or Heat-Set?* on page 57 for more about working with crystals.)

2 Trim the fusible web so it is slightly smaller than the finished bookmark, excluding the fringe. Place the embroidered bookmark face down on a thickly folded towel. Center the fusible web over the back of the bookmark, adhesive side down, and press to adhere according to manufacturer's instructions. When cool, remove the paper backing.

3 Trim felt to the same size as the bookmark, excluding the fringe. Lay it over the fusible web on the back of the bookmark and press to adhere.

Close-Up of *Iris*

Orchid Band for Journal Cover

Turn a simple black-covered journal into a lovely personal diary
with this embroidered orchid design. The decorative band is easy to
assemble. Add some pretty ribbons and a unique button that match
your embroidery for a nice finish.

MATERIALS

DESIGN FROM CD-ROM
0605, *Orchid*

SUPPLIES & TOOLS
9" × 12" (22.9cm × 30.5cm) piece
white cotton fabric (for embroidery)

9" × 12" (22.9cm × 30.5cm) piece
iron-on interfacing

1 yd. (91.4cm) pink ribbon, $\frac{3}{8}$"
(9mm) wide

½ yd. (45.7cm) pink ribbon, ¼"
(6mm) wide

1 decorative button (size/style
appropriate for journal design)

One 5" × 7" (12.7cm × 17.8cm)
black-covered journal

Embroidery and bobbin threads

Iron

Permanent fabric glue

Removable marking tool

Tear-away stabilizer

EMBROIDER THE DESIGN

1 Print the Thread and Design Guide for *Orchid* from the CD-ROM. Transfer the design to your embroidery machine.

2 Following manufacturer's instructions, fuse the interfacing to the white fabric wrong side. Fold the white fabric in half horizontally and vertically to determine the center. With a removable marking tool, place cross marks on the fabric at the center of the motif position.

3 Hoop the interfaced fabric and stabilizer. To center the design, align the cross marks on the fabric with the centerlines on the hoop. Use the machine controls to position the needle over the cross marks.

4 Embroider the design.

5 When stitching is complete, trim the jump stitches, remove the fabric from the hoop and tear away the excess stabilizer.

FINISH THE JOURNAL COVER

1 To create the cover band, trim the finished embroidery to 4" × 12" (10.2cm × 30.5cm), leaving about ¾" (1.9cm) fabric at either side of the band and about 3¾" (9.5cm) at the top and bottom.

2 Place the embroidered band on the front cover ½" (1.3cm) from the spine of the journal, centering the design vertically. Fold the excess top and bottom fabric to the inside of the front cover and finger crease both folds. Adhere the band to the front cover with permanent fabric glue; also glue the ends of the band on the inside of the front cover. Make sure the glue on the inside front cover is dry before closing the journal. **Tip:** Slide a piece of waxed paper between the inside cover and the pages to prevent sticking as the glue dries.

Close-Up of *Orchid*

3 Cut the ⅜" (9mm) ribbon in half. Glue it along the long raw edges of the fabric, overlapping the fabric edge about ¼" (6mm) and extending to the inside front cover. If you wish, cover the short ends of the white fabric on the inside front cover in the same manner.

4 Cut the ¼" (6mm) ribbon in half. Glue one piece at the center right edge of the front cover and the other piece at the center left edge of the back cover. Glue a decorative button over the ribbon end on the front cover.

Japanese Maple Leaves Pillow

Choose the soft autumn palette presented here or embroider these colorful maple leaves to coordinate with your own décor. These motifs would also work well on table linens; or, as a treat for yourself, try tumbling them down the length of a soft wool scarf to keep you warm in a late October chill.

MATERIALS

DESIGNS FROM CD-ROM
0606, *Maple Leaf 1* (small)

0607, *Maple Leaf 2* (medium)

0608, *Maple Leaf 3* (large)

SUPPLIES & TOOLS
White linen envelope pillowcase with hemstitched detail (project uses a hemstitched lingerie bag from All About Blanks, see *Resources*, page 126)

1 pillow form, 12" × 12" (30.5cm × 30.5cm), or a size that fits the pillowcase you're using

1 skein embroidery floss, 6-strand cotton in the same tone as the machine embroidery

Embroidery and bobbin threads

Adhesive tear-away stabilizer

1 large-eyed needle (for floss)

Removable marking tool

Straight pins or painter's tape (for positioning template)

Template paper or other material

EMBROIDER THE DESIGN

1 Print the Thread and Design Guide for three *Japanese Maple Leaf* designs (small, medium and large) from the CD-ROM. Transfer the designs to your embroidery machine.

2 Create templates for one leaf in each size. Find and mark the center and top of each template. Randomly position the three leaves as desired on the pillow flap, rotating them as desired, or use the photo of the finished pillow on this page as your guide. Pin or tape the templates in place.

3 Hoop the adhesive stabilizer and expose or activate the adhesive. Adhere the portion of the flap to be embroidered first to the stabilizer, aligning the cross marks on the template with the centering marks on the hoop. Note that the pillow flap may be hooped at an angle. Use the machine controls to position the needle over the cross marks. Remove the template before embroidering.

4 Embroider each design, stabilizing and re-hooping for each leaf.

5 When stitching is complete, trim the jump stitches, remove the embroidery from the hoop and tear away the excess stabilizer.

Close-Up of *Japanese Maple Leaves*
On the project, the positioning of the motifs is medium (upper left), large (center) and small (upper right).

FINISH THE PILLOWCASE

1 Thread a large-eyed needle with undivided six-strand embroidery floss; pull a length of floss loose from the skein but do not cut.

2 Weave the needle and floss in and out of the hemstitched edge to create a coordinating border on the pillowcase flap. Pull additional floss from the skein as needed.

3 When the entire length of hemstitching has been threaded with floss, take the needle to the flap's underside. Use the needle to knot the floss securely around the last weave on the underside of the flap, then cut the floss close to the knot.

4 Cut the floss from the skein, leaving a tail long enough to thread on the needle. Knot this tail securely around the first weave on the underside of the pillowcase flap, then cut the floss close to the knot.

5 Insert the pillow form. Bring the embroidered flap down over the front of the pillow.

CHAPTER 7

KOI & DRAGONFLY

No Japanese garden would be complete without a glistening pool alive with swimming koi and hovering dragonflies. Sparkling like a trail of gemstones beneath the water, the koi flash by in shades of brilliant orange, opalescent white and silken black. This marvelous creature is known as *nishikigoi* in Japanese, which means *shimmering jewel*. The celebration of Children's Day on May 5th includes a display of brightly colored koi banners dancing in the doorways of Japan, bringing joy, strength and courage to the children that live there.

The iridescent wings of dragonflies come in many colors. My favorites have wings that seem woven from magical threads of turquoise and sapphire. In the late afternoons of a Vermont summer, they gather by the stream in a daily ritual. It's mesmerizing to watch as they dance and dart in every direction. They depart in the closing light only to return again the next afternoon. Perhaps this is where their legend takes form, for the dragonfly is a symbol of immortality and regeneration.

The two circular designs of the dragonfly and koi make up into lovely towel borders and spa accessories. What a delightful way to relax and bring a free-flowing calming energy to your bath or pool.

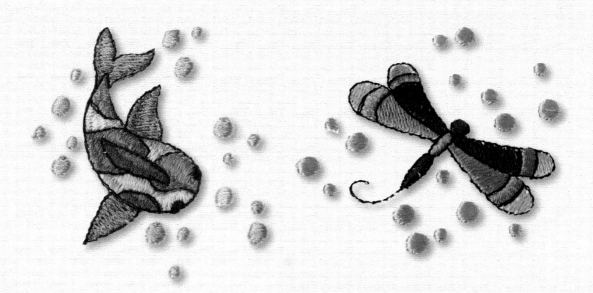

Koi & Dragonfly Towels

You can duplicate the graceful movement and gentle energy of the koi and dragonfly on your towels. For larger-sized towels, use your machine's touch screen to repeat the motifs; your software might allow you to mirror and rotate the designs as you like.

MATERIALS

DESIGNS FROM CD-ROM
0701, *Koi*

0702, *Dragonfly*

SUPPLIES & TOOLS
Two 11" × 18" (30cm × 46cm) terry velour fingertip towels (project towels from The Sewphisticated Stitcher, see *Resources*, page 126)

Embroidery and bobbin threads for each design

Straight pins or painter's tape (for positioning template)

Tear-away stabilizer

Template paper or other material

Temporary spray adhesive

Water-soluble topping

EMBROIDER THE DESIGN

1 Print the Thread and Design Guides for *Koi* and *Dragonfly* from the CD-ROM. Transfer the designs to your embroidery machine.

2 To plan the design placement, create a template for each motif. Your software might allow you to mirror the motifs for your templates. Find and mark the center of each template with cross marks.

3 Using spray adhesive, secure water-soluble topping to the surface of the towel over the area you plan to embroider.

4 Fold the towel in half vertically and in half vertically again to find the three centerlines for the motifs; the horizontal center of each motif is 2" (5.1cm) above the fringed edge of the towel.

5 Hoop the towel, stabilizer and topping, aligning the cross marks on the first template with the centering marks on the hoop. Use the machine controls to position the needle over the cross marks. Remove the template before you begin stitching.

6 Embroider the design, stabilizing and re-hooping for each motif.

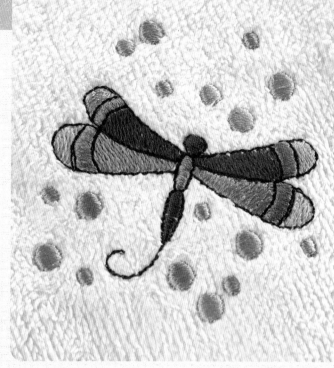

Close-Up of *Dragonfly*

7 When stitching is complete for each design, trim the jump stitches, remove the towel from the hoop and tear away the excess stabilizer.

8 Carefully tear away as much water-soluble topping as possible. Remove the remaining topping according to manufacturer's instructions.

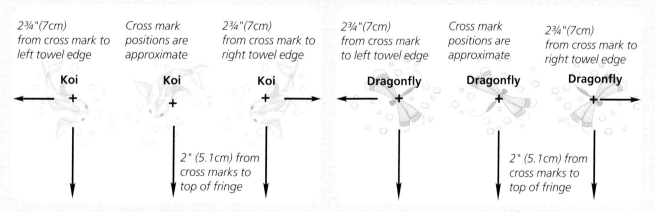

2¾"(7cm) from cross mark to left towel edge   *Cross mark positions are approximate*   *2¾"(7cm) from cross mark to right towel edge*   *2¾"(7cm) from cross mark to left towel edge*   *Cross mark positions are approximate*   *2¾"(7cm) from cross mark to right towel edge*

Koi   **Koi**   **Koi**   **Dragonfly**   **Dragonfly**   **Dragonfly**

2" (5.1cm) from cross marks to top of fringe   *2" (5.1cm) from cross marks to top of fringe*

Placement Diagram for *Koi Towel*
The center koi is rotated 90° clockwise. The right koi is flipped horizontally (left/right).

Placement Diagram for *Dragonfly Towel*
The left dragonfly is flipped horizontally (left/right) and rotated 90° counterclockwise. The right dragonfly is rotated 90° clockwise.

Koi Slippers

After a relaxing massage or a soothing bath, slip your toes into a pair of soft slippers embroidered with playful koi. Wouldn't these make a fun gift for a workout partner or your best friend at the spa?

MATERIALS

DESIGN FROM CD-ROM
0701, *Koi*

SUPPLIES & TOOLS

1 pair white terry velour spa slippers (project slippers* from The Sewphisticated Stitcher, see *Resources*, page 126)

Embroidery and bobbin threads

Cut-away stabilizer

Removable marking tool

Straight pins or painter's tape (for positioning template)

Template paper or other material

Temporary spray adhesive

Water-soluble topping

These slippers are constructed with a hook and loop closure, making it easier to position each slipper for embroidery.

EMBROIDER THE DESIGN

1 Print the Thread and Design Guide for *Koi* from the CD-ROM. Transfer the design to your embroidery machine.

2 To plan the design placement of the koi, create two templates, one flipped horizontally to create a mirror image (the right slipper koi is used as is, the left slipper koi is flipped). Your software might allow you to mirror the motif for your templates. Find and mark the center of each template.

3 With spray adhesive, secure the water-soluble topping to the surface of the slipper area you will be embroidering. Pin or tape the template into place.

4 Hoop the stabilizer and spray it with temporary adhesive. Open the slipper's hook and loop fastener and arrange the slipper instep on the sticky stabilizer surface, aligning the template cross marks with the centerlines on the hoop. The left slipper sole should extend to the left of the hoop and the right slipper sole to the right of the hoop, with the toes pointed toward the operator once the hoop is in place. Use the machine controls to position the needle over the cross marks.

5 Embroider the design.

6 After stitching is complete, trim the jump stitches, remove the slipper and stabilizer from the hoop and cut away the excess stabilizer. Tear away as much water-soluble topping as possible.

7 Repeat Steps 4–6 for the second slipper.

8 Remove the remaining water-soluble topping according to manufacturer's instructions.

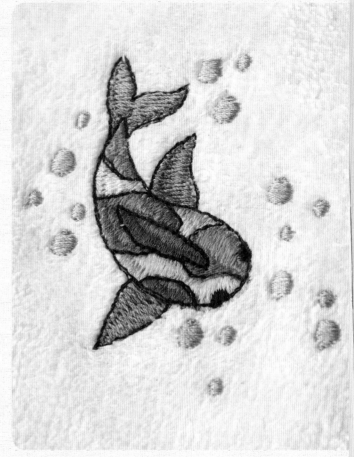

Close-Up of *Koi*
Note that this motif is flipped horizontally (left/right) for the left slipper.

CHAPTER 8

BIRDS & BLOSSOMS

The celebration of Sakura Matsuri, the annual cherry blossom festival, inspired this chapter. The delicate blossoms of the cherry tree open for a brief time every spring. Their fleeting beauty brings to mind the precious qualities of life—its fragility and the promise of things to come—as the sweet petals fall like a pink snowstorm.

   Among the many birds perched in the tree branches, we find the tiny chickadee sharing a message of courage and hope. He has braved the cold winter and is now part of this renewed season, ready to restart his life's yearly cycle. The images of birds and blossoms are wonderful for machine embroidery.

   I've designed two different *Bird & Blossoms* motifs and two border elements so you can make up some lovely spring table linens. Expand the ensemble by combining the motifs on your own to create placemats, napkin rings, coasters or any number of additional projects. These designs would also look very pleasing as borders on bed linens and towels.

Chickadee Trivet

This ready-made trivet is simple to assemble and will protect your table from that pot of hot tea. Here's a thought: Purchase a plain tea cozy and embroider it with the second chickadee (*Bird & Blossoms 2*). Pack up the trivet, cozy and a special box of your favorite tea, tie it with a bow and you'll have the perfect hostess or shower gift.

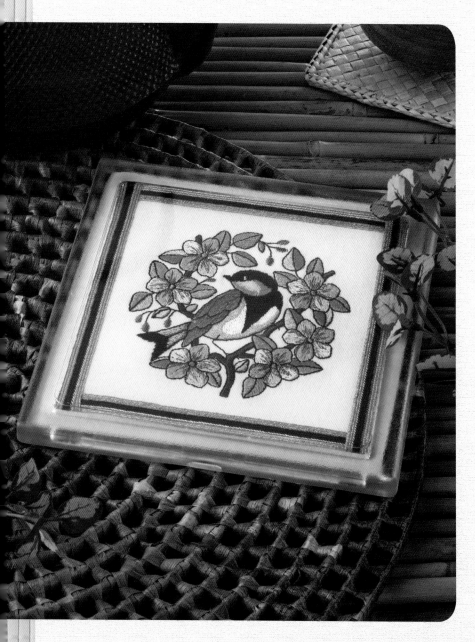

MATERIALS

DESIGN FROM CD-ROM
0801, *Bird & Blossoms 1*

SUPPLIES & TOOLS
One 12" × 12" (30.5cm × 30.5cm) piece white cotton cloth

One 6" × 6" (15.2cm × 15.2cm) acrylic trivet (project trivet from MCG Textiles, see *Resources*, page 126)

One 10" × 10" (25.4cm × 25.4cm) piece interfacing, medium weight

1 yd. (91.4cm) black/gold ribbon, 3/8" (9mm) wide

Embroidery and bobbin threads

Iron

Permanent fabric glue

Removable marking tool

Tear-away stabilizer

PREPARE THE FABRIC

1 Print the Thread and Design Guide for *Bird & Blossoms 1* from the CD-ROM. Transfer the design to your embroidery machine.

2 Following the manufacturer's instructions, fuse the interfacing to the white fabric's wrong side.

3 Hoop the interfaced fabric and stabilizer, roughly centering the fabric in the hoop.

4 Embroider the design.

5 When stitching is complete, trim the jump stitches, remove the fabric from the hoop and tear away the excess stabilizer.

FINISH THE TRIVET

1 Trim the embroidered fabric to 5" × 5" (12.7cm × 12.7cm), being sure to keep the embroidery at the center. You can use the cardboard backing that comes with the trivet as your template.

2 Cut four 5" (12.7cm) lengths of ribbon and glue them along all four sides of the embroidered fabric to hide the raw edges. Overlap the ends as shown in the photo on this page.

3 Insert the embroidery into the trivet, making sure it's smooth and centered. Snap in the backing that comes with the trivet.

Close-Up of *Bird & Blossoms 1*
Purchase two trivets and embroider Bird & Blossoms 2 *as well—you'll have a set of chickadees to brighten and protect your table.*

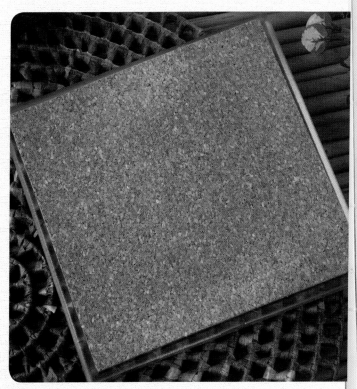

Underside of Trivet
Commercial trivets made especially for showcasing needlework usually come with backing material that simply snaps or slides into place—no gluing necessary!

Spring Table Topper

Combine the *Bird & Blossoms* chickadees and the side and center border designs to make a charming table topper that brings the spirit of springtime indoors. Follow my diagram on page 89 for laying out the elements, or sketch out a plan of your own using your templates.

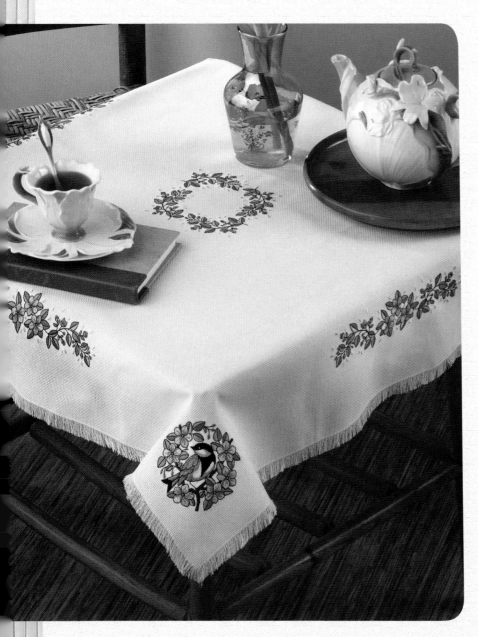

MATERIALS

DESIGNS FROM CD-ROM

0801, *Bird & Blossoms 1*

0802, *Bird & Blossoms 2*

0803, *Bird & Blossoms Center Border*

0804, *Bird & Blossoms Side Border*

SUPPLIES & TOOLS

One 33" × 33" (84cm × 84cm) piece 14 count Royal Classic Aida cloth (project fabric by Charles Craft, Inc., see *Resources*, page 126)

Embroidery and bobbin threads

Sewing thread (white)

Cut-away stabilizer

Removable marking tool

Sewing machine (if your embroidery machine doesn't sew)

Straight pins or painter's tape (for positioning templates)

Template paper or other material

Temporary spray adhesive (optional)

PREPARE THE FABRIC

1 Using white sewing thread, stitch a line seven threads from the raw edge of the Aida cloth along all four sides.

2 To create a fringe, pull the fabric's threads from all four sides, from the raw edge to the stitching line.

EMBROIDER THE DESIGN

1 Print the Thread and Design Guides for *Bird & Blossoms 1* and *2*, *Center Border* and *Side Border* from the CD-ROM. Transfer the designs to your embroidery machine.

2 Fold the fringed Aida cloth horizontally and vertically to find and mark the centers, then lay the cloth out on a flat surface. See the diagram on page 89 to determine the appropriate number of templates to create for design placement. Your embroidery software might allow you to mirror and rotate the motifs for each template.

  Create templates for all of the motifs. Find and mark the center and top of each template. See *Creating the Border Garland* on page 88 for tips on combining the *Center Border* and *Side Border* motifs.

3 Beginning with the first motif you plan to embroider, pin or tape the template into place according to the diagram or your own design plan.

4 Fold the fabric in half lengthwise and press to crease the vertical centerline. Repeat to fold and crease the horizontal centerline. Fold the fabric in half diagonally and crease to mark the diagonal centerline. Unfold and refold on the diagonal between the other two corners to mark the second diagonal centerline. If necessary, lightly sketch the centerlines with a removable marking tool so they are easily visible.

Close-Up of *Spring Table Topper* Corner
Note that the corner motifs are positioned 2¾" (7cm) from the stitched line (not the fringe ends) to the center of the motif.

5 Beginning with the center garland, referring to the diagram on page 89 for placement measurements and design orientation, hoop fabric and stabilizer and embroider design 0804 (*Bird & Blossoms Side Border*) four times, re-hooping with fresh stabilizer for each motif. The top of each motif should lie toward the tablecloth center. **Note:** It may be simpler to hoop cut-away stabilizer, spray it with temporary adhesive and attach the fabric with the diagonal line and cross mark aligned with the hoop's centerlines.

6 Next, embroider each motif in the side garlands. Where the diagram indicates *0804R*, use design 0804 flipped side to side (reversed). See the sidebar for more information.

7 Now embroider the corner motifs, aligning the hoop's centerlines with the diagonal line and cross mark at each corner.

8 When stitching is complete, trim the jump stitches, remove the cloth from the hoop and cut away the excess stabilizer.

Creating the Border Garland

The border garlands for *Spring Table Topper* are created by combining the *Center Border* and *Side Border* motifs. If desired, create templates with template paper or vellum so you can see the previously embroidered motifs as you position each element. Refer to the diagram on page 89 for additional details. Where the diagram indicates *0804R*, use design 0804 (*Bird & Blossoms Side Border*) flipped side to side (reversed).

Stitch the *Center Border* motif first, then the two *Side Border* motifs positioned so they appear joined to the *Center Border*. If a large hoop is available, stitch two or even all three parts of the garland in one hooping.

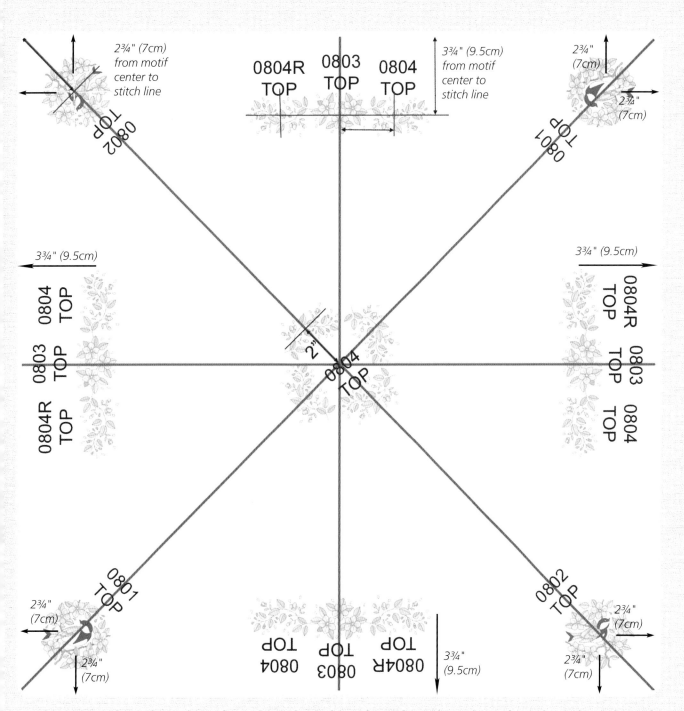

2¾" (7cm) from motif center to stitch line

0804R TOP   0803 TOP   0804 TOP

3¾" (9.5cm) from motif center to stitch line

2¾" (7cm)   2¾" (7cm)

0802 TOP   0801 TOP

3¾" (9.5cm)   3¾" (9.5cm)

0804 TOP   0803 TOP   0804R TOP

0804R TOP   0803 TOP   0804 TOP

2"   0804 TOP

0801 TOP   0802 TOP

2¾" (7cm)   2¾" (7cm)   2¾" (7cm)   2¾" (7cm)

0804 TOP   0803 TOP   0804R TOP   3¾" (9.5cm)

Design Placement Diagram for *Spring Table Topper*

Bird & Blossoms Napkins

Matching napkins add a lovely touch while you sip your tea on a fragrant spring afternoon. Although the project calls for two napkins, purchase as many as you need and embroider as many of either design as desired. For a more elaborate design, add *Bird & Blossoms Center Border* or *Bird & Blossoms Side Border* along the sides of the napkins.

MATERIALS

DESIGNS FROM CD-ROM
0801, *Bird & Blossoms 1*

0802, *Bird & Blossoms 2*

SUPPLIES & TOOLS
2 prefinished napkins in 14 count Royal Classic Aida cloth (project cloth by Charles Craft, Inc., see *Resources*, page 126)

Embroidery and bobbin threads

Iron-on cut-away mesh stabilizer

Removable marking tool

EMBROIDER THE DESIGN

1 Print the Thread and Design Guides for *Bird & Blossoms 1* and *Bird & Blossoms 2* from the CD-ROM. Transfer the designs to your embroidery machine.

2 Fold one napkin in half diagonally, dividing the corner to be embroidered, and crease lightly. Mark the diagonal crease with a removable marking tool, then measure and draw a cross mark 4½" (10.2cm) above the top of the fringe to locate the embroidery center point.

3 Cut a piece of iron-on cut-away mesh stabilizer large enough to fill the hoop. Lay the napkin face down, oriented diagonally on the ironing board. Cover with the stabilizer, adhesive side down and oriented straight. Press to fuse. The stabilizer will extend beyond the napkin edges, making the project large enough to hoop.

4 Hoop the stabilized napkin, aligning the cross marks on the napkin with the centerlines on the hoop. Use the machine controls to position the needle over the cross marks.

5 Embroider the design.

6 When stitching is complete, trim the jump stitches, remove the napkin from the hoop and cut away the excess stabilizer.

7 Repeat Steps 2–6 for *Bird & Blossoms 2* and the second napkin.

Close-Up of *Bird & Blossoms 2*

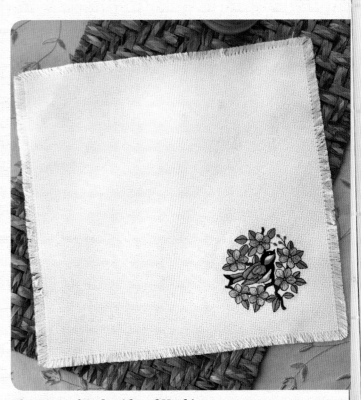

Flat View of Embroidered Napkin
*Note that the motif is positioned in the corner 4"
(10.2cm) from the corner point of the fringe to the
center of the motif.*

CHAPTER 9

Calligraphic Symbols

In China, the skilled artistry of the calligrapher is considered a sacred gift. As a high form of creative expression, calligraphy is practiced in an environment of serenity and peace. Graceful brush strokes speak from the heart of the artist. These abstract symbols are known as *kanji* in Japan. With black ink and handcrafted brushes, the calligrapher creates a freestyle movement that carries the words in a harmonious rhythm, sending messages of enlightenment and wisdom.

   One word in Japanese calligraphy combines different images. For example, the symbol for happiness is a combination of strokes for the mouth, a cultivated field and a stroke symbolizing *united in heaven*. Happiness: *to fill from a source of abundance.*

   I've provided four special symbols on the CD-ROM for you to embroider. With a stark palette of black and gold, they will look wonderful sewn on many of the Asian-style patterns available in the fabric shops today. Three of the symbols appear in the projects for this chapter. *Happiness Kanji Symbol* and *Peace Kanji Symbol* make beautifully expressive cards (page 94). The *Kanji Banner* (page 97) embroidered on pretty Asian-inspired cottons would be wonderful in an entryway to wish peace, happiness and harmony to all who enter.

Kanji Symbols Cards

Symbols in the emotive brush strokes of the calligrapher make lovely embroidered cards. Not only will you be sending wishes for peace and happiness, but you will also be creating lasting keepsakes that can be mounted easily in a frame for a thoughtful display.

MATERIALS

DESIGNS FROM CD-ROM
0901, *Happiness Kanji Symbol*

0903, *Peace Kanji Symbol*

SUPPLIES & TOOLS

Happiness Kanji Symbol card:

One 9" × 9" (22.9cm × 22.9cm) square gold cotton batik cloth

One 6" × 6" (15.2cm × 15.2cm) square iron-on interfacing, medium weight

12" (30.5cm) black velvet ribbon, ¼" (6mm) wide

1 decorative button (size/style appropriate for card design)

One 5" × 5" (12.7cm × 12.7cm) cream square tri-fold card with 3½" (8.9cm) round die cut window*

Peace Kanji Symbol card:

One 9" × 9" (22.9cm × 22.9cm) square purple cotton batik cloth

One 6" × 6" (15.2cm x 15.2cm) square iron-on interfacing, medium weight

12" (30.5cm) black/gold ribbon, ⅜" (9mm) wide

1 decorative button (size/style appropriate for card design)

One 5" × 5" (12.7cm × 12.7cm) gold square tri-fold card with 3½" (8.9cm) round die cut window*

For both cards:

Double-sided tape

Embroidery and bobbin threads

Iron

Iron-on tear-away stabilizer

Permanent fabric glue

*(project cards by Impress Cards, see *Resources*, page 126)

EMBROIDER THE DESIGNS

1 Print the Thread and Design Guides for *Happiness Kanji Symbol* and *Peace Kanji Symbol* from the CD-ROM. Transfer the designs to your embroidery machine.

2 Center the iron-on interfacing, adhesive side down, on the wrong side of the *Happiness Kanji Symbol* fabric. Press to fuse following manufacturer's instructions.

3 Now, following manufacturer's instructions, fuse a piece of iron-on tear-away stabilizer large enough to fill the hoop to the wrong side of the interfaced fabric, centering the fabric on the stabilizer.

4 Hoop the stabilized fabric, roughly centering it in the hoop.

5 Embroider the design.

6 When stitching is complete, trim the jump stitches, remove the fabric from the hoop and tear away the excess stabilizer.

7 Follow Steps 2–6, substituting *Peace Kanji Symbol* and corresponding fabric.

Close-Up of *Happiness Kanji Symbol*

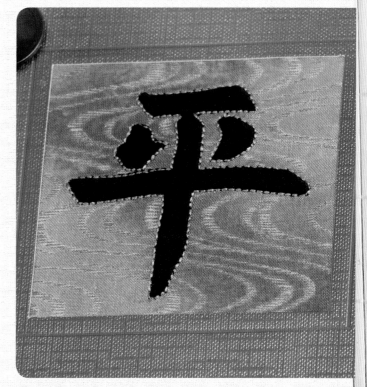

Close-Up of *Peace Kanji Symbol*

FINISH THE CARDS

1 Trim each embroidered fabric to 4½" x 4½" (11.4cm x 11.4cm), keeping the design centered.

2 Apply double-stick tape along the edges of the die cut window on the wrong side of the card front. (Be sure not to close the tri-fold flap over the tape.)

3 Turn the open card over and center the window over the embroidered design, making sure the fabric is smooth and the design is oriented correctly on the card front. Press the card down firmly to adhere. Add a few spots of glue along the edge of the left tri-fold flap, fold it over the section with the embroidery and press to adhere.

4 Beginning approximately ¾" (1.9cm) from the upper left edge of the front of the card, glue ribbon ⅜" (9mm) from the fold, bringing it over the card top and down near the inside fold, then back up the front.

5 Glue a decorative button where the ribbon ends meet on the front of the card.

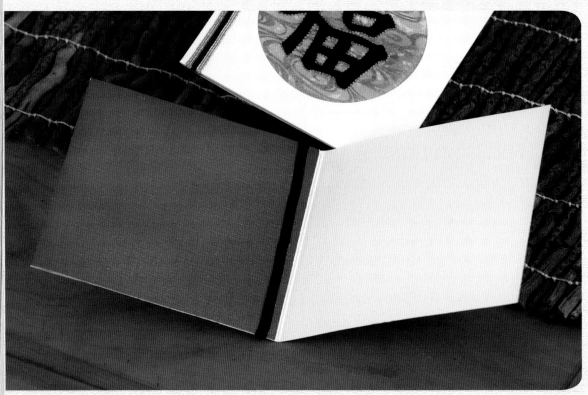

Interior of Card

Using a tri-fold card makes it easy to give the card interior a finished look. With the right side of the embroidery face down, simply fold the left flap over the back of the embroidered piece and glue the corners (do not apply glue where it will touch the embroidery). Apply the ribbon to the card after the flap has been glued.

Kanji Banner

Perfect for welcoming guests or inviting positive energy into your home, this kanji banner is quick to make. A simple bamboo rod adds to the Asian spirit of the project and makes it easy to hang this banner above your threshold or to grace any room. Finished size: 7¼" × 19¼" (18.4cm × 48.9cm), excluding tabs.

MATERIALS

DESIGNS FROM CD-ROM

0901, *Happiness Kanji Symbol*

0902, *Harmony Kanji Symbol*

0903, *Peace Kanji Symbol*

SUPPLIES & TOOLS

Two 9" x 9" (22.9cm x 22.9cm) squares dark gold cotton cloth (for *Peace Kanji Symbol* and *Harmony Kanji Symbol* panels)

One 9" x 9" (22.9cm x 22.9cm) square of pale gold cotton cloth (for *Happiness Kanji Symbol* panel)

1 yd. (91.4cm) black print fabric (sashing, borders, backing and finishing)

One 8" x 20" (20.3cm x 50.8cm) piece fusible fleece

1 yd. (91.4m) gold satin cord

Two 21" (53.3cm) lengths bamboo* (for hanging rod)

Embroidery and bobbin threads

Iron

Iron-on tear-away stabilizer

Needle for hand sewing

Permanent fabric glue

Sewing machine (if your embroidery machine doesn't sew)

Sewing thread (colors to match fabrics)

Available at garden centers and easily cut with a small hand saw.

EMBROIDER THE DESIGNS

1 Print the Thread and Design Guides for *Peace Kanji Symbol*, *Happiness Kanji Symbol* and *Harmony Kanji Symbol* from the CD-ROM. Transfer the designs to your embroidery machine.

2 Cut a piece of iron-on tear-away stabilizer large enough to fill the hoop. Following manufacturer's instructions, center the stabilizer on the wrong side of the *Peace Kanji Symbol* fabric and press.

3 Hoop the stabilized fabric, roughly centering the fabric in the hoop.

4 Embroider the design.

5 When stitching is complete, trim the jump stitches, remove the fabric from the hoop and tear away the excess stabilizer.

6 Repeat Steps 2–5 for *Happiness Kanji Symbol* and *Harmony Kanji Symbol* on their corresponding fabrics.

Close-Up of *Harmony Kanji Symbol*

FINISH THE BANNER

1 Trim each embroidered panel to 6" × 6" (15.2cm × 15.2cm), with each design centered in its square.

2 For hanging tabs, cut three 2" × 6" (5.1cm × 15.2cm) rectangles from the black print fabric. Fold the tabs in half lengthwise and machine stitch along the long edge using a ¼" (6mm) seam. Turn each tab to the right side. Flatten the tab with the seam line centered and press.

3 Cut four 2" × 6" (5.1cm × 15.2cm) strips for the vertical sashing on the front of the banner. With right sides facing and using a ¼" (6mm) seam, join one strip to each edge of the *Peace Kanji Symbol* panel and to each edge of the *Harmony Kanji Symbol* panel.

4 With right sides facing and using a ¼" (6mm) seam, join the left side of the *Happiness Kanji Symbol* panel to the right black sashing strip on the *Peace Kanji Symbol* panel. Join the right side of the *Happiness Kanji Symbol* panel to the left black sashing strip on the *Harmony Kanji Symbol* panel. Press each seam toward the sashing.

5 Cut two 2" × 20" (5.1cm × 50.8cm) strips of black printed fabric for the top and bottom borders. With right sides facing and using a ¼" (6mm) seam, join the strips to the top and bottom (long edges) of the banner. Press each seam toward the border strips.

6 Match the adhesive side of the fusible fleece to the wrong side of the banner. Cover the embroidery with a press cloth and iron to fuse according to manufacturer's instructions.

7 Fold the three finished tabs in half, concealing the seam within the fold. With raw edges matching along the top of the banner, position the tabs at the center top and 2" (5.1cm) from each end. Baste into place with the tab folds toward the center of the banner front.

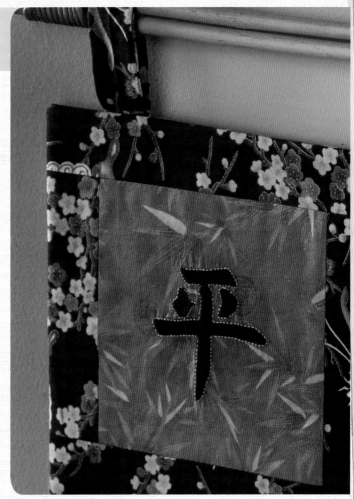

Panel and Construction Detail
Black print sashing frames and joins the embroidered panels.

8 Cut an 8" × 20" (20.3cm × 50.8cm) piece of backing fabric. Place this on top of the banner with right sides facing. With a ¼" (6mm) seam, sew all around the layered banner, catching the tab raw edges in the seam and leaving a gap along the bottom edge for turning.

9 Clip the corners and turn the banner right side out. Press the edges firmly and slipstitch the bottom gap closed.

10 To make a hanging rod, hold the two lengths of bamboo together and wind satin cord around them near each end. Add a dab of permanent fabric glue to secure the cord in place. Slip the rod through the tabs on the banner and hang.

CHAPTER 10

Symbols of Longevity: Butterflies

Brightly colored butterflies dancing among the garden flowers are a joyful sign of summer. The artists of China, ever aware of the natural world around them, used the image of lilting butterflies in many of their decorative arts. Often seen as symbols of longevity, butterflies are known as *hu-tieh* in Mandarin, the name literally meaning seventy years.

Gemstone hues—rich purple, bright green, deep blue, shimmering pink and gold—colored the fluttering wings of silk and bamboo butterfly kites. These were flown across the summer sky or hung in homes to bring good health and long life. In scroll paintings, the butterfly was often depicted with inspirational words written in delicate calligraphy, suggesting that the words were lifted on the gentle breeze of the butterfly's flight.

I've designed three different butterfly motifs for you to mix, match, resize and play with to your heart's delight. (See *Resizing Tip* on page 15.) Use these motifs individually to create cards with a special message of your own, or group them together for a bold statement on a cheerful tote. These designs would be wonderful on many ready-made items, too. Picture them on summer table linens or some brightly colored beach towels. Set your creative spirit free and let it fly!

Butterfly Greeting Cards

Symbolic of a long and healthy life, these colorful butterflies create charming cards, perfect for sending happy birthday wishes to a friend or loved one. They also make ideal get well cards, or special tokens to say "thinking of you."

MATERIALS

DESIGNS FROM CD-ROM
1002, *Butterfly 2*

1003, *Butterfly 3*

SUPPLIES & TOOLS

Butterfly 2 card:

One 9" × 9" (22.9cm × 22.9cm) square green cotton batik cloth

One 6" × 6" (15.2cm x 15.2cm) square iron-on interfacing, medium weight

12" (30.5cm) purple satin ribbon, ¼" (6mm) wide

1 decorative coin (check jewelry supply and embellishment departments at needlework and craft stores)

One 5" × 5" (12.7cm × 12.7cm) gold square tri-fold card with 3½" (8.9cm) round diecut window*

Butterfly 3 card:

One 9" × 9" (22.9cm × 22.9cm) square pink cotton batik cloth

One 6" × 6" (15.2cm x 15.2cm) square iron-on interfacing, medium weight

One 5" × 5" (12.7cm × 12.7cm) gold square tri-fold card with 3½" (8.9cm) round die cut window*

12" (30.5cm) length dark blue ribbon, 3⁄16" (5mm) wide

4 small satin butterflies (available at craft and needlework stores or online)

For both cards:

Embroidery and bobbin threads

Double-sided tape

Iron

Permanent fabric glue

Removable marking tool

Tear-away stabilizer

*(project cards by Impress Cards, see *Resources*, page 126)

EMBROIDER THE DESIGNS

1 Print the Thread and Design Guides for *Butterfly 2* and *Butterfly 3* from the CD-ROM. Transfer the designs to your embroidery machine.

2 Center the iron-on interfacing, adhesive side down, on the wrong side of the *Butterfly 2* fabric. Press to fuse following manufacturer's instructions.

3 Cut a piece of iron-on tear-away stabilizer large enough to fill the hoop. Following manufacturer's instructions, fuse the stabilizer to the wrong side of the interfaced fabric, centering the fabric on the stabilizer.

4 Hoop the stabilized fabric, roughly centering it in the hoop.

5 Embroider the design.

6 When stitching is complete, trim the jump stitches, remove the fabric from the hoop and tear away the excess stabilizer.

7 Follow Steps 2–6, substituting *Butterfly 3* and corresponding fabric.

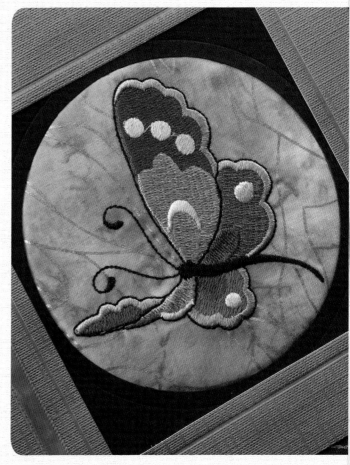

Close-Up of *Butterfly 2*

FINISH THE CARDS

1 Rotate the butterfly motif within the card's window to determine a pleasing position. Lightly mark the top center on the embroidery wrong side so it will not show in the finished card. Remove the embroidery.

2 Trim the embroidery to 4½" x 4½" (11.5cm x 11.5cm), keeping the design at the center of the square and orienting the motif as determined in Step 2.

3 Open the card completely and lay it face down. Apply double-stick tape along the edges of the diecut window on the wrong side of the card front. (Be sure not to close the tri-fold flap over the tape.)

4 Turn the open card over and center the window over the embroidered design, positioning the butterfly motif as in Step 1 and making sure the fabric is smooth. Press the card down firmly to adhere.

5 Beginning approximately ¾" (1.9cm) from the upper left edge of the front of the card, glue ribbon ⅜" (9mm) from the fold, bringing it over the card top and down near the inside fold, then back up the front.

6 Glue a decorative coin where the ribbon ends meet on the front of the *Butterfly 2* card. For the *Butterfly 3* card, glue one of the satin butterflies where the ends of the ribbon meet; randomly scatter the others around the design as desired (see the photo on this page for suggested placement).

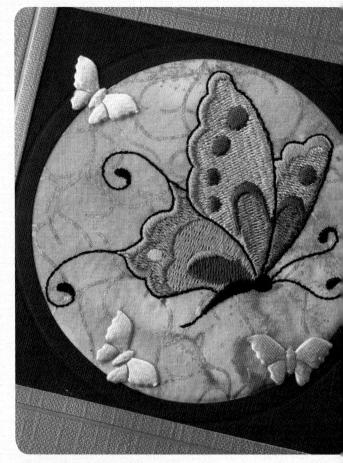

Close-Up of *Butterfly 3 Card*
Glue a scattering of satin butterflies as shown here, or arrange them as you prefer. Be sure to glue one butterfly over the ends of the ribbon in the upper left-hand corner.

Breezy Butterfly Summer Tote

Create this fun tote for carrying all your vacation essentials. It's the perfect size for stowing your summer reading, sunglasses and sunscreen, or use it to tuck away your latest sewing projects. Finished size: 11½" × 14" (29.2cm × 35.6cm), excluding the handles.

MATERIALS

DESIGNS FROM CD-ROM
- 1001, *Butterfly 1*
- 1002, *Butterfly 2*
- 1003, *Butterfly 3*

SUPPLIES & TOOLS
- One 12" × 12" (30.5cm × 30.5cm) square background fabric (for embroidered panel)
- ½ yd. (45.7cm) background fabric (for lining and handles)
- ½ yd. (45.7cm) coordinating fabric (for bag)
- ½ yd (45.7cm) fusible fleece
- 10 embroidered flowers (optional) (available in craft and needlework stores or online)
- Embroidery and bobbin threads
- Iron
- Permanent fabric glue
- Removable marking tool
- Sewing machine (if embroidery machine doesn't sew)
- Sewing thread to match fabrics
- Tear-away stabilizer

EMBROIDER THE DESIGN

1 Print the Thread and Design Guides for *Butterfly 1*, *Butterfly 2* and *Butterfly 3* from the CD-ROM. Transfer the designs to your embroidery machine.

2 Create templates of the three butterfly designs and mark the horizontal and vertical centerlines on each. Also mark the top of each motif. With a removable marking tool, lightly draw an 8½" (21.6cm) high × 6½" (16.5cm) wide rectangle at the center of the fabric and randomly position the three butterflies to your liking within the area; use the photos on pages 105 and 107 as your guide. Pin or tape the templates in place.

3 Hoop the fabric and stabilizer for the first motif you plan to embroider. To center the design, align the cross marks on the fabric with the centerlines on the hoop. Rotate the fabric to match the template's orientation, or hoop the fabric straight and use the machine controls to rotate the design relative to the hoop.

4 Embroider the first design.

5 When stitching is complete, trim the jump stitches, remove the fabric from the hoop and tear away the excess stabilizer.

6 Repeat Steps 3–5 for each of the other two butterfly designs.

Close-Up of *Butterfly 1*

MAKE THE TOTE BAG

1 For the bag's center front panel, trim the embroidered fabric square to 8" × 10" (20.3cm × 25.4cm), leaving a ¾" (1.9cm) fabric allowance between the edges of the panel and the butterflies.

2 Cut two strips of coordinating fabric 2½" × 10" (6.3cm × 25.4cm). With right sides together and raw edges matched, stitch a strip to each side of the embroidered panel. Press the seams toward the coordinating fabric strips.

3 Cut two strips of coordinating fabric 2½" × 12½" (6.3cm × 31.7cm). With right sides together, sew one strip to the top and one to the bottom of the bag front. Press the seams toward the coordinating fabric strips.

4 For the bag back, cut a piece of coordinating fabric 14" × 12" (35.6cm x 30.5cm).

5 Cut two pieces of background fabric 1½" × 12" (3.8cm × 30.5cm). With right sides together, sew one strip to the top of the pieced bag front and the other strip to the top of the bag back.

6 Cut two pieces of fusible fleece 15" × 12" (38.1cm × 30.5cm). Fuse the fleece to the wrong sides of the bag front and back, following manufacturer's instructions. Use a press cloth to protect the embroidery.

7 With right sides together, sew the bag front to the bag back along the sides and bottom using a ½" (1.3cm) seam.

8 Cut two pieces of background fabric 15" × 12" (38.1cm × 30.5cm) for the bag lining. With right sides together, sew the lining pieces together along the sides and bottom, leaving a 5" (12.7cm) gap in the bottom seam for turning.

9 To make the handles, cut two strips of coordinating fabric 1½" × 22" (3.8cm × 55.9cm). Fold each strip in half lengthwise with right sides together and stitch along the long edge. Turn the strips right side out and press flat, with the seam along one fold.

Positioning of Butterflies on the Tote Bag
Follow the positioning of butterflies as shown here, or mirror and rotate the motifs to create your own design.

10 Position the ends of one strip on the top edge of the bag front, with each end 2½" (6.3cm) from the side seam, the handle raw edges extending ¼" (6mm) beyond the bag's upper raw edge. Be sure the handle is not twisted. Pin into place. Repeat to position the second handle on the bag back.

11 Place the bag, right side out, inside the lining, wrong side out, with the raw edges matching. The right sides will be together with the handles sandwiched in between the bag and lining and extending beyond the bag raw edges. Stitch ¼" (6mm) from the upper edge, catching the handles in the seam.

12 Turn the bag right side out through the gap in the lining seam. Tuck the lining into the bag and press. Topstitch ¼" (6mm) from the bag's upper edge and close the gap in the lining with hand or machine stitches.

If you like, scatter some ready-made embroidered flowers over the front of the bag to give an extra breezy feel to your tote. Use permanent fabric glue to fix the flowers into place.

Index to Designs on CD-Rom

Chapter One: Floral Fans

0101, *Iris Fan*
3.22″ × 4.78″ (8.2cm × 12.1cm)
13 thread changes

0102, *Magnolia Fan*
3.19″ × 4.81″ (8.1cm × 12.2cm)
17 thread changes

0103, *Peony Fan*
3.22″ × 4.82″ (8.2cm × 12.2cm)
18 thread changes

Chapter Two: The Japanese Garden

0201, *Bellflower Crest*
2.80" × 2.81" (7.1cm × 7.1cm)
7 thread changes

0202, *Chrysanthemum Crest*
2.77" × 2.77" (7.0cm × 7.0cm)
7 thread changes

0203, *Paulownia Crest*
2.82" × 2.81" (7.2cm × 7.1cm)
7 thread changes

0204, *Peony Crest*
2.85″ × 2.85″ (7.2cm × 7.2cm)
8 thread changes

0205, *Plum Blossom Crest*
2.82″ × 2.82″ (7.2cm × 7.2cm)
19 thread changes

Chapter Three: Playful Pandas

0301, *Panda 1*
3.80″ × 3.78″ (10.0cm × 9.6cm)
13 thread changes

0302, *Panda 2*
3.80″ × 3.78″ (10.0cm × 9.6cm)
11 thread changes

0303, *Panda 3*
3.83″ × 3.78″ (9.7cm × 9.6cm)
12 thread changes

0304, *Panda 4*
3.82″ × 3.78″ (9.7cm × 9.6cm)
14 thread changes

0305, *Panda 5*
3.80″ × 3.78″ (10.0cm × 9.6cm)
13 thread changes

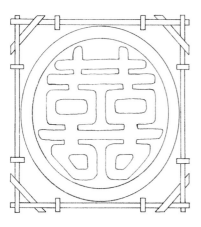

0306, *Double Happiness Symbol*
3.78″ × 3.78″ (9.6cm × 9.6cm)
4 thread changes

Chapter Four: Pagoda & Geisha

0401, *Blue Pagoda*
3.61″ × 3.61″ (9.2cm × 9.2cm)
8 thread changes

0402, *Geisha*
4.29" × 4.30" (10.9cm × 10.9cm)
16 thread changes

Chapter Five: Four Seasons Kimonos

0501, *Summer Kimono*
4.20" × 3.08" (10.7cm × 7.8cm)
24 thread changes

0502, *Spring Kimono*
4.76" × 3.39" (12.1cm × 8.6cm)
20 thread changes

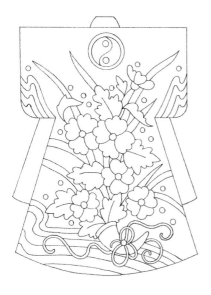

0503, *Autumn Kimono*
4.18″ × 3.08″ (10.6cm × 7.8cm)
18 thread changes

0504, *Winter Kimono*
4.25″ × 3.05″ (10.8cm × 7.7cm)
20 thread changes

Chapter Six: Flowers of Ancient Culture

0601, *Oriental Poppy 1*
2.57″ × 2.10″ (6.5cm × 5.3cm)
3 thread changes

0602, *Oriental Poppy 2*
3.09″ × 1.83″ (7.8cm × 4.6cm)
3 thread changes

0603, *Oriental Poppy 3*
3.07″ × 2.34″ (7.8cm × 5.9cm)
3 thread changes

0604, *Iris*
6.62″ × 2.01″ (16.8cm × 5.1cm)
14 thread changes

0605, *Orchid*
6.26″ × 2.35″ (15.9cm × 6.0cm)
21 thread changes

0606, *Japanese Maple 1 (Small)*
2.56" × 2.14" (6.5cm × 5.4cm)
1 thread change

0607, *Japanese Maple 2 (Medium)*
3.27" × 2.96" (8.3cm × 7.5cm)
1 thread change

0608, *Japanese Maple 3 (Large)*
4.53" × 3.80" (11.5cm × 9.6cm)
1 thread change

Chapter Seven: Koi & Dragonfly

0701, *Koi*
2.46" × 2.49" (6.2cm × 6.3cm)
11 thread changes

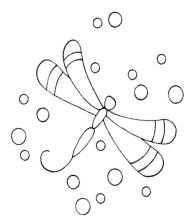

0702, *Dragonfly*
2.55" × 2.57" (6.5cm × 6.5cm)
10 thread changes

Chapter Eight: Birds & Blossoms

0801, *Bird & Blossoms 1*
3.62" × 3.59" (9.2cm × 9.1cm)
15 thread changes

0802, *Bird & Blossoms 2*
3.46" × 3.47" (8.8cm × 8.8cm)
16 thread changes

0803, *Bird & Blossoms Center Border*
2.06" × 2.86" (5.2cm × 7.3cm)
8 thread changes

0804, *Bird & Blossoms Side Border*
1.90" × 3.15" (4.8cm × 8.0cm)
7 thread changes

Chapter Nine Calligraphic Symbols

0901, *Happiness Kanji Symbol*
2.60" × 2.56" (6.6cm × 6.5cm)
2 thread changes

0902, *Harmony Kanji Symbol*
2.58" × 2.59" (6.5cm × 6.6cm)
2 thread changes

0903, *Peace Kanji Symbol*
2.59" × 2.58" (6.6cm × 6.5cm)
2 thread changes

0904, *Tranquility Kanji Symbol*
2.47" × 2.15" (6.3cm × 5.5cm)
2 thread changes

Chapter Ten Symbols of Longevity: Butterflies

1001, *Butterfly 1*
3.17" × 3.34" (8.0cm × 8.5cm)
9 thread changes

1002, *Butterfly 2*
3.15" × 3.07" (8.0cm × 7.8cm)
7 thread changes

1003, *Butterfly 3*
2.75" × 3.14" (7.0cm × 8.0cm)
9 thread changes

DMC Floss List for Hand Embroidery

The following pages list the DMC six-strand cotton floss required to work each of the designs on the CD-ROM that accompanies this book. Numbers and colors are provided for each so you can substitute other kinds of floss, if desired. For most designs, one skein of each required color should be sufficient.

These lists are also provided individually by project on the CD-ROM so they can be printed out for reference while shopping and while working the designs.

0101, IRIS FAN

DMC #	COLOR
155	Medium dark blue violet
166	Medium light moss green
310	Black
312	Very dark baby blue
350	Medium coral
435	Very light brown
581	Moss green
3746	Dark blue violet
3820	Dark straw

0102, MAGNOLIA FAN

DMC #	COLOR
310	Black
312	Very dark baby blue
350	Medium coral
415	Pearl gray
435	Very light brown
581	Moss green
712	Cream
728	Topaz
Blanc	White

0103, PEONY FAN

DMC #	COLOR
155	Medium dark blue violet
166	Medium light moss green
310	Black
320	Medium pistachio green
435	Very light brown
602	Medium cranberry
603	Cranberry
605	Very light cranberry
809	Delft blue
3820	Dark straw
Blanc	White

0201, BELLFLOWER CREST

DMC #	COLOR
580	Dark moss green
581	Moss green
798	Dark Delft blue
809	Delft blue
833	Light golden olive
895	Very dark hunter green
3364	Pine green

0202, CHRYSANTHEMUM CREST

DMC #	COLOR
471	Very light avocado green
563	Light jade
726	Light topaz
833	Light golden olive
895	Very dark hunter green
972	Deep canary
988	Medium forest green

0203, PAULOWNIA CREST

DMC #	COLOR
553	Violet
581	Moss green
833	Light golden olive
895	Very dark hunter green
988	Medium forest green
3837	Dark rosewood

0204, PEONY CREST

DMC #	COLOR
601	Dark cranberry
603	Cranberry
605	Very light cranberry
702	Kelly green
703	Chartreuse
833	Light golden olive
895	Very dark hunter green
907	Light parrot green

0205, PLUM BLOSSOM CREST

DMC #	COLOR
415	Pearl gray
580	Dark moss green
581	Moss green
833	Light golden olive
895	Very dark hunter green
3364	Pine green
Blanc	White

0301, PANDA 1

DMC #	COLOR
310	Black
317	Pewter gray
415	Pearl gray
581	Moss green
733	Medium olive green
3852	Very dark straw
Blanc	White

0302, PANDA 2

DMC #	COLOR
310	Black
317	Pewter gray
415	Pearl gray
581	Moss green
733	Medium olive green
3852	Very dark straw
Blanc	White

0303, PANDA 3

DMC #	COLOR
310	Black
317	Pewter gray
415	Pearl gray
581	Moss green
733	Medium olive green
3852	Very dark straw
Blanc	White

0304, PANDA 4

DMC #	COLOR
310	Black
317	Pewter gray
415	Pearl gray
581	Moss green
733	Medium olive green
3852	Very dark straw
Blanc	White

0305, PANDA 5

DMC #	COLOR
310	Black
317	Pewter gray
415	Pearl gray
581	Moss green
733	Medium olive green
3852	Very dark straw
Blanc	White

0306, DOUBLE HAPPINESS SYMBOL

DMC #	COLOR
310	Black
3852	Very dark straw

0401, BLUE PAGODA

DMC #	COLOR
797	Royal blue
798	Dark Delft blue
800	Pale Delft blue
809	Delft blue

0402, GEISHA

DMC #	COLOR
310	Black
553	Violet
597	Turquoise
602	Medium cranberry
816	Garnet
907	Light parrot green
3770	Very light tawny
3852	Very dark straw
Blanc	White

0501, SUMMER KIMONO

DMC #	COLOR
166	Medium light moss green
310	Black
581	Moss green
603	Cranberry
809	Delft blue
3364	Pine green
3829	Very dark old gold
3852	Very dark straw
Blanc	White

0502, SPRING KIMONO

DMC #	COLOR
166	Medium light moss green
310	Black
553	Violet
554	Light violet
809	Delft blue
921	Copper
3364	Pine green
3829	Very dark old gold
3852	Very dark straw
Blanc	White

0503, AUTUMN KIMONO

DMC #	COLOR
310	Black
581	Moss green
602	Medium cranberry
604	Light cranberry
798	Dark Delft blue
809	Delft blue
3363	Medium pine green
3364	Pine green
3821	Medium mustard
3929	Very dark old gold
Blanc	White

0504, WINTER KIMONO

DMC #	COLOR
208	Very dark lavender
310	Black
312	Very dark baby blue
415	Pearl gray
434	Light brown
603	Cranberry
704	Bright chartreuse
809	Delft blue
3364	Pine green
3829	Very dark old gold
3852	Very dark straw
Blanc	White

0601, ORIENTAL POPPY 1

DMC #	COLOR
310	Black
666	Bright red
701	Light green

0602, ORIENTAL POPPY 2

DMC #	COLOR
310	Black
666	Bright red
701	Light green

0603, ORIENTAL POPPY 3

DMC #	COLOR
310	Black
666	Bright red
701	Light green

0604, IRIS

DMC #	COLOR NAME
166	Medium light moss green
312	Very dark baby blue
322	Dark dark baby blue
340	Medium blue violet
581	Moss green
895	Very dark hunter green
3746	Dark blue violet
3852	Very dark straw

0605, ORCHID

DMC #	COLOR
166	Medium light moss green
312	Very dark baby blue
322	Dark dark baby blue
581	Moss green
602	Medium cranberry
603	Cranberry
605	Very light cranberry
895	Very dark hunter green
3820	Dark straw

0606, JAPANESE MAPLE 1
(Small)

DMC #	COLOR
783	Medium topaz

0607, JAPANESE MAPLE 2
(Medium)

DMC #	COLOR
301	Medium mahogany

0608, JAPANESE MAPLE 3
(Large)

DMC #	COLOR
3777	Very dark terra cotta

0701, KOI

DMC #	COLOR NAME
310	Black
317	Pewter gray
318	Light steel gray
415	Pearl gray
741	Medium tangerine
947	Burnt orange
3325	Light baby blue
3811	Very light turquoise
Blanc	White

0702, DRAGONFLY

DMC #	COLOR NAME
310	Black
341	Light blue violet
435	Very light brown
775	Very light baby blue
823	Dark navy blue
827	Very light blue
959	Medium seagreen
964	Light seagreen
3852	Very dark straw

0801, BIRD & BLOSSOMS 1

DMC #	COLOR NAME
310	Black
317	Pewter gray
318	Light steel gray
433	Medium brown
562	Medium jade
677	Very light old gold
703	Chartreuse
746	Off white
961	Dark dusty rose
963	Ultra very light dusty rose
3716	Very light dusty rose

0802, BIRD & BLOSSOMS 2

DMC #	COLOR NAME
310	Black
317	Pewter gray
318	Light steel gray
433	Medium brown
562	Medium jade
677	Very light old gold
703	Chartreuse
746	Off white
961	Dark dusty rose
963	Ultra very light dusty rose
3716	Very light dusty rose

0803, BIRD & BLOSSOMS
CENTER BORDER

DMC #	COLOR NAME
310	Black
433	Medium brown
562	Medium jade
703	Chartreuse
961	Dark dusty rose
963	Ultra very light dusty rose
3716	Very light dusty rose

0804, BIRD & BLOSSOMS
SIDE BORDER

DMC #	COLOR NAME
310	Black
433	Medium brown
562	Medium jade
703	Chartreuse
961	Dark dusty rose
963	Ultra very light dusty rose
3716	Very light dusty rose

0901, HAPPINESS KANJI
SYMBOL

DMC #	COLOR NAME
310	Black
3852	Very dark straw

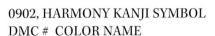

0902, HARMONY KANJI SYMBOL

DMC #	COLOR NAME
310	Black
3852	Very dark straw

0903, PEACE KANJI SYMBOL

DMC #	COLOR NAME
310	Black
3852	Very dark straw

0904, TRANQUILITY KANJI SYMBOL

DMC #	COLOR NAME
310	Black
3852	Very dark straw

1001, BUTTERFLY 1

DMC #	COLOR NAME
208	Very dark lavender
310	Black
553	Violet
581	Moss green
958	Dark seagreen
3819	Light moss green
3820	Dark straw
Blanc	White

1002, BUTTERFLY 2

DMC #	COLOR NAME
310	Black
553	Violet
798	Dark Delft blue
809	Delft blue
958	Dark seagreen
3819	Light moss green
3820	Dark straw

1003, BUTTERFLY 3

DMC #	COLOR NAME
310	Black
553	Violet
581	Moss green
798	Dark Delft blue
809	Delft blue
958	Dark seagreen
3819	Light moss green
3820	Dark straw

About the Author

Joan Elliott has been creating needlework designs for more than 30 years. Her titles for David & Charles include *A Cross Stitcher's Oriental Odyssey* (2004), *Cross Stitch Teddies* (2007), *Cross Stitch Sentiments and Sayings* (2007), *Native American Cross Stitch* (2005), *Cross Stitch Wit & Wisdom* (2007), *A Woman's World in Cross Stitch* (2007), *Bewitching Cross Stitch* (2009) and her newest, *Cross Stitch Greetings* (2010). *Asian-Inspired Machine Embroidery* is Joan's first book of designs for Krause Publications.

Joan divides her time between Brooklyn, New York, and Vermont, where she indulges her passion for gardening and shares the many joys and experiences of city and country life with her husband.

Web site: joanelliottdesign.com

Blog: http://joanelliott.wordpress. com/category/whats-new/

Resources

Here you will find wonderful sources for threads, fabrics and all the bits and bobs necessary for making up the projects in this book. Many thanks to these manufacturers for providing all the supplies that helped make this book possible. Please note that my two UK resources are easily accessed via the Internet and both provide prompt delivery.

ALL ABOUT BLANKS
866-425-2657
www.allaboutblanks.com
(*embroidery blanks, including linen cocktail napkins, mosaic stitch hankie and hemstitched lingerie bag*)

BLUMENTHAL LANSING COMPANY
www.buttonsplus.com
(*trims, ribbons and buttons*)

CHARLES CRAFT, INC.
800-277-0980
www.charlescraft.com
(*Monaco fabric, 14 count Royal Classic Aida cloth and prefinished items for machine embroidery, including 18 count white Aida bookmarks*)

DMC CORPORATION
973-589-0606
www.dmc-usa.com
(*embroidery threads and stranded cotton floss*)

IMPRESS CARDS (UK)
01493 441166
www.impresscards.com
(*blank greeting cards*)

KANDI CORPORATION
800-985-2634
www.kandicorp.com
(*heat-set crystals*)

KREINIK MANUFACTURING
800-537-2166
www.kreinik.com
(*metallic threads*)

LAND'S END
www.landsend.com
(*child's nightgown*)

MCG TEXTILES
www.mcgtextiles.com
(*accessories for mounting needlework, including acrylic trivets*)

PEARL RIVER
www.pearlriver.com
(*pink brocade blouse*)

POLSTITCHES DESIGNS (UK)
01559 370406
www.polstitchesdesigns.co.uk
(*hand-dyed evenweave and Aida fabrics*)

ROBISON-ANTON TEXTILE COMPANY
800-847-3235
www.robison-anton.com
(*Super Strength™ Rayon threads*)

RUBIN MUSEUM OF ART
www.rmanyc.org
(*silk scarf*)

THE SEWPHISTICATED STITCHER
www.thesewphisticatedstitcher.com
1866 210 0072
(*embroidery blanks, including bright lime tote bag, key lime visor, black 3-pocket apron, premium velour fringed finger tip towels and terry spa slippers*)

SUDBERRY HOUSE
860-388-9045
www.sudberryhouse.com
(*items for mounting embroidery, including wooden keepsake boxes and hand mirrors*)

SULKY OF AMERICA
www.sulky.com
800-874-4115
(*machine embroidery products including stabilizers, threads and adhesives*)

THE WARM COMPANY
800-234-WARM
www.warmcompany.com
(*batting and interfacing*)

ZWEIGART
732-562-8888
www.zweigart.com
(*linen, evenweave and Aida fabrics and white cotton Anne cloth*)

Index

Expand your machine embroidery knowledge and skills!

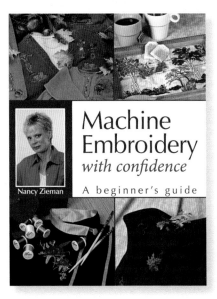

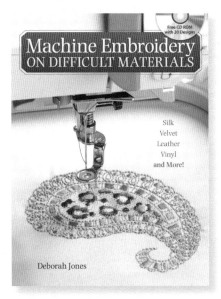

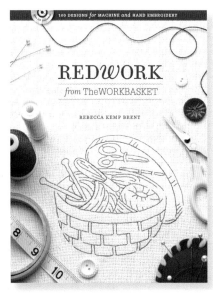

Machine Embroidery with Confidence
A Beginner's Guide
Nancy Zieman

Machine Embroidery on Difficult Materials
Silk, Velvet, Leather, Vinyl and More!
Deborah Jones

Redwork from The WORKBASKET
100 Designs for Machine and Hand Embroidery
Rebecca Kemp Brent

Nancy Zieman, the nation's most recognized and revered sewing expert, covers everything you need to know to master machine embroidery in this essential guide. An easy-to-understand tutorial explains the basics of machine embroidery, and detailed photos depict every step of using these machines for top-notch results. Learn about tools, different types of machines, designs, templating/positioning, software, stabilizers, hooping, fabrics, problem shooting and finishing touches.

Take your machine embroidery to new heights by working with materials readily found, but often overlooked because they pucker and run, buckle and stretch, break your thread or bury your embroidery in mounds of plush pile. With the author's expert advice, you can embroider even the most challenging materials with consistently beautiful results. The accompanying CD-ROM includes 14 embroidery designs in 38 fabric-specific versions so that you can use the settings as reference for other designs.

Achieve the look of vintage redwork embroidery with your embroidery machine. *Redwork from The WORKBASKET* presents 100 authentic *WORKBASKET* designs on CD-ROM, digitized in multiple formats for machine embroidery. Designs are provided in JPEG and PDF formats so hand-embroiderers can create their own transfers. Twelve projects show how to incorporate these designs to make dishtowels, framed sentiments, tote bags, a bed quilt and more.

paperback; 128 pages; #CFEM
ISBN-10: 0-87349-857-7
ISBN-13: 978-0-87349-857-9

paperback; 128 pages; #Z2050
ISBN-10: 0-89689-654-4
ISBN-13: 978-0-89689-654-3

paperback; 128 pages; #Z3839
ISBN-10: 0-89689-972-1
ISBN-13: 978-0896899728